Leading American Businesses

**Profiles of Major American Companies
and the People Who Made Them Important**

Leading American Businesses

volume
2
G-L

**Profiles of Major American Companies
and the People Who Made Them Important**

U·X·L®

THOMSON
—★—™
GALE

Detroit • New York • San Diego • San Francisco • Cleveland • New Haven, Conn. • Waterville, Maine • London • Munich

Leading American Businesses
Profiles of Major American Companies and the People Who Made Them Important

Michael Burgan
Taryn Benbow-Pfalzgraf, Kenneth R. Wells, Kelle S. Sisung

Project Editor
Elizabeth Grunow

Imaging and Multimedia
Robyn V. Young

Composition
Evi Seoud

Permissions
Lori Hines

Product Design
Jennifer Wahi

Manufacturing
Rita Wimberley

LIBRARY OF CONGRESS CATALOGING-IN-PUBLICATION DATA

Benbow-Pfalzgraf, Taryn.
Leaders of American business / Taryn Benbow-Pfalzgraf, Michael Burgan, and Kenneth R. Wells ; Elizabeth Grunow, editor.
    p. cm.
        Summary: A collection of forty-five biographies of Americans who have achieved great success and had a great impact in the world of business, plus in-depth company profiles and shorter biographical sketches. Includes bibliographical references and index.
        ISBN 0-7876-5428-0 (hardcover : set : alk. paper) — ISBN 0-7876-5429-9 (v. 1) — ISBN 0-7876-5430-2 (v. 2) — ISBN 0-7876-5431-0 (v. 3)
        1. Businesspeople—United States—Biography. 2. United States—Biography. 3. Business enterprises—United States—Directories. 4. Corporations—United States—Directories. [1. Businesspeople. 2. United States—Biography. 3. Business enterprises.] I. Burgan, Michael. II. Wells, Kenneth R., 1950–. III. Grunow, Elizabeth Shaw. IV. Title.

HC102.5.A2 B46 2002
338.092'2–dc21

2002004270

Printed in the United States of America
10 9 8 7 6 5 4 3 2 1

Contents

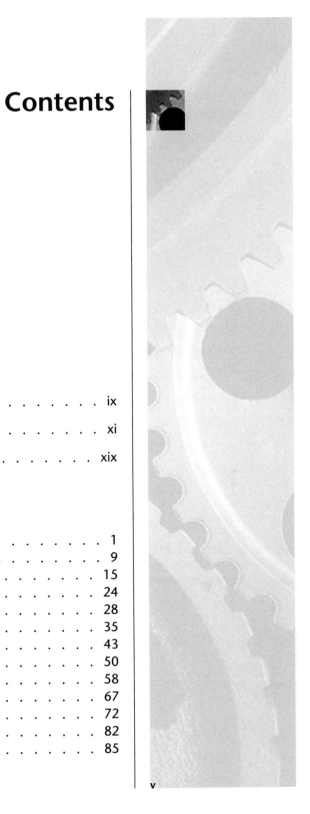

Volume 2 (G–L)

Volume 3 (M–Z)

Reader's Guide

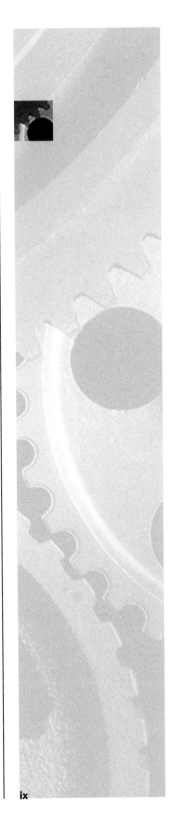

L *eading American Businesses: Profiles of Major American Companies and the People Who Made Them Important* focuses on forty-five of today's most successful and influential corporations. Some of these companies have their roots in the nineteenth century, while others are less than a decade old. Some were created by merging existing companies, while others sprung from the talents of only one person. Whatever their differences, these businesses have one thing in common: they represent the best of the energized, creative spirit that has shaped the American economy for more than 165 years.

Each entry in *Leading American Businesses* includes a history of the company with essential information about its current operations as well as profiles of its founders and other key figures. Entries also contain "At a Glance" sidebar boxes highlighting facts about the company and a timeline specific to that company. The three-volume set contains more than 170 black-and-white photos, and each volume includes a glossary, a general timeline of American business, and an index of the subjects discussed throughout *Leading American Businesses*.

Acknowledgments

The editor would like to thank Karen Raugust and Jodi Essey-Stapleton for additional writing and copy editing work for this set.

The editor would also like to acknowledge the expert business review and advice of Anneliese J. Shaw of MORPACE International, Inc.

Suggestions Are Welcome

We welcome your comments on *Leading American Businesses: Profiles of Major American Companies and the People Who Made Them Important.* Please write, Editors, *Leading American Businesses,* U•X•L, 27500 Drake Road, Farmington Hills, MI 48331-3535; call toll-free: 1-800-877-4253; fax to 248-414-5043; or send e-mail via http://www.galegroup.com.

Words to Know

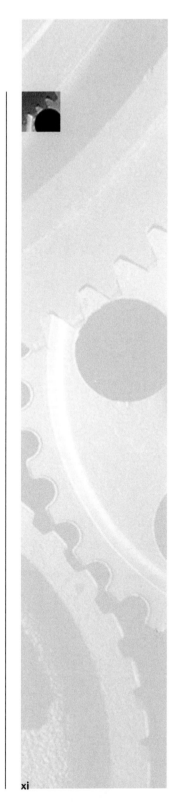

A

Acquisition: Some thing or entity that a company comes into possession or control of.

Administration: The act of directing or managing the affairs of a business.

Advertising: Promotion of a product or service through use of commercial space in mediums such as television, billboards, newspapers, or magazines.

Ambition: Strong desire to achieve something.

Annual sales: Amount of money made by a company per year.

Antitrust: Putting an end to or regulating business monopolies that are considered to not be in the best interest of the economy or the public.

Apparel: Clothing.

Apprentice: Someone who works with a "master" to learn a trade.

Assets: Property subject to the payment of debts.

Assembly line: An operation that has something being put together in pieces by traveling down some sort of conveyor from person to person or machine to machine.

B

Baby Boomer: The generation born between 1946 and 1964.

Bankruptcy: When a person or business is declared legally unable to pay their debts. In return, all of the person's goods and properties must be sold off in order to pay as much of their debt as possible.

Benefits: Financial incentives provided by employers to draw workers to the company.

Board of directors: A committee of business professionals that oversees the running of a company.

Brand: Goods identified by a name as the product of a single manufacturer.

Browser: A computer program used with the Internet to make it easier to look up information.

Bureaucracy: A business administration in which the need to follow rules and regulations complicates and slows effective completion of work.

C

Capitalism: An economic system that is driven by prices being set based upon the supply and demand for goods and services, and where the competition between businesses drives the economy.

Cargo: Freight carried by a ship, plane, or other vehicle.

Catalogue: In the case of retail businesses, a bound booklet with pictures, decriptions, and prices of things for sale.

Chain: A group of similar businesses under a single ownership.

Chairman of the board: The head of the board of directors for a company or organization.

Chief executive officer (CEO): The top executive in a company or organization.

Child labor: Employing people who are younger than the set age allowed for legal employment, often at a lower pay rate.

Commerce: The buying or selling of goods.

Communism: A system of government through which the people all share equally the goods produced by the community and the services provided by the government.

Competition: Rivalry between businesses for the same customers.

Conglomerate: An association of companies.

Consultant: Person who gives expert or professional advice.

Consumer: A person who buys or uses goods or services.

Consumer advocate: A person who speaks out for a group of consumers, bringing attention to problems or inadequacies to make sure that the consumers' concerns are being heard and addressed.

Controlling interest: When one person or group of people owns enough shares of a company that they can control the outcome of shareholder votes.

Corporate raider: An individual or business that works to gain controlling interest in a business in order to take over the management of that business.

Corporation: A group of people who have legally defined themselves as a singular entity under one name, and can act as a single person rather than a group.

Credit: A system for the purchase of goods with the understanding that they will be paid off over time.

D

Debt: Something owed from one person or entity to another. Also, owing more than one has (for instance, owing $100 when one has only $50 means that they are in debt).

Deregulate: To remove restrictions from.

Direct sales: When a business goes straight to the customer rather than waiting for the customer to visit a store or

Web site or use a catalog. Door-to-door sales is a method of direct sales.

Discount: Reduction made from the regular price of a product.

Downturn: Decreasing business or marketing activity.

Dry-goods: Products such as textiles, clothing, hardware goods, and groceries.

E

Economy: Production, development, and management system of wealth in a country, region, or business.

Entrepreneur: Person who runs a business enterprise and takes on the risks involved.

F

Forgery: Illegal production of something that is false.

Foundation: Organization established by a gift of money with certain provisions.

Franchise: A business agreement through which an independent person (or group of people) can own and operate a business under the parent company's name, and the parent company educates them in retailing, what to sell, and how much to charge.

G

Generic brand: The branding of the product produced by the store itself. A generic brand is usually sold at a cheaper price than a name brand.

The Great Depression: A period between 1929 and 1934, starting with the stock market crash in 1929 in the United States, characterized by extremely low economic activity throughout most of the world. It forced the closure of many businesses, found many people out of meaningful work, and left some homeless.

H

Headquarters: Center of operations.

I

Income: Monetary gain from capital or labor.

Incorporation: The filing of papers to be a public company, adding "Inc." to the company's name, choosing a board of directors, and installing officers such as president, vice president, and treasurer to run the business and answer to the board of directors.

Industry: Manufacture or production of goods on a large scale.

Innovation: Introduction of something new.

Invention: Something produced or created by using the imagination.

Inventory: Products carried by a company.

Investment: Putting money into property, stocks, or business to make a profit.

Investor: A person or group that buys shares of a company.

L

Labor strike: Protest by workers who stop work to force an employer to agree with demands.

Labor union: A large group of people joined together for the purpose of ensuring fair working conditions and pay rates for their members.

Lay off: A dismissal of employees because there is not enough work to be done.

License: When a company allows other companies to use their name, products, or characters as a part of their product or marketing. For instance, Disney licenses its characters to be used on Hallmark greetings cards.

Lobbyist: People who try to convince lawmakers to vote favorably on issues that affect the company or industry for which they work.

M

Manufacture: Act or process of producing something.

Market: The business of buying and selling products.

Market research: Studying customers and their buying habits to understand which products sell better and why.

Mass production: To make something in large quantities, usually on an assembly line.

Merchandise: Goods bought and sold in business.

Merger: Usually the union of two or more companies, corporations, or organizations.

Monopoly: Exclusive possession, control, or ownership.

Multimedia: Using several media, such as video, music, lighting, computers, etc.

N

New Deal: The programs and policies for economic recovery and social reform introduced during the 1930s by President Franklin D. Roosevelt.

Nonprofit organization: An organization set up to produce a good or service but not to make money off of that product.

O

Occupation: A job.

P

Parent company: A large company that owns and oversees several smaller companies.

Patent: A grant made by the government that assures an inventor the exclusive right to ownership (for the purposes of manufacture, use, or sale) of a given invention for a set amount of time.

Philanthropy: Desire or effort to aid other humans, usually by making donations to charities.

Pioneer: Person who develops new areas of research or thought.

Private: A private company is one that is owned by a select group of people, such as a family.

Profit: Money made from a product after expenses and taxes are removed.

Profit margin: The difference between the price a company pays for a good and the price at which they sell it. For instance, Home Depot may buy fans at $27 a piece and sell them at $30 a piece, making their profit margin $3.

Profit-sharing: A bonus system in which workers are given money based on how much money a company makes in a given period of time.

Public: When a company sells shares on the New York Stock Exchange, usually to grow the company.

R

Ration: To limit the amount of some good over a period of time.

Recession: An economic downturn that forces companies to cut jobs and consumers to invest less money.

Recruit: To supply with new employees.

Research and development: A segment of manufacturing in which businesses find ways to use science to create scientifically advanced products.

Retail: The sale of small items in small quantities.

Revenue: Income through the sale of goods, services, or properties.

Royalties: Payment to an author or composer for each copy of a work sold.

S

Slogan: A phrase used repeatedly to advertise a product or service.

Spokesperson: A well-known personality who appears in commercials or ads promoting a product or service.

Stock: Money or capital invested or available for investment or trading.

Stock split: When a company realizes that its stock price has risen to a level that is too expensive for the average investor, they decide to split the stock and each single share becomes a double share, costing half as much.

Stockbroker: A person who buys and sells stocks and bonds for a client and receives a commission.

Subsidiary: A company that is wholly or partially owned by another.

T

Technology: Use of scientific knowledge to solve industrial and commercial problems.

Trade deficit: When a country buys more goods from foreign nations than it sells to foreign nations.

Trademark: Legal device showing the ownership of merchandise.

U

Union: Organization of workers formed to advance its members' interests in wages, benefits, and working conditions.

V

Venture capitalist: A person or group of people who invest in businesses that are risky or have a low likelihood of return on their investment, yet if successful will yield a great deal of profit.

Vertically integrated: When a business owns other companies that produce the primary products needed to produce their main product. (If an auto company owned a steel mill, a tire company, and an engine building facility, they would be a vertically integrated business.)

W

Wholesale: Sale of goods in large quantity, usually at a lower cost.

Timeline of American Business

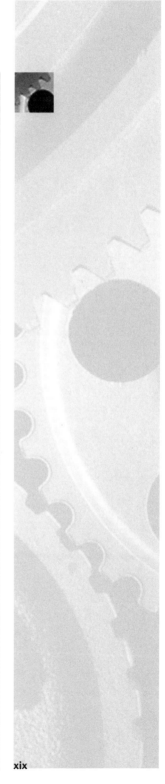

1837: William Procter and James Gamble create the Procter & Gamble Company.

1850: Henry Wells and William Fargo form the American Express Company.

1873: Levi Strauss & Company sells its first pair of riveted blue jeans.

1876: Alexander Graham Bell receives the first telephone patent.

1877: Bell Telephone Company is formed.

1879: Procter & Gamble launch Ivory bar soap.

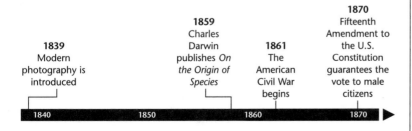

1839
Modern photography is introduced

1859
Charles Darwin publishes *On the Origin of Species*

1861
The American Civil War begins

1870
Fifteenth Amendment to the U.S. Constitution guarantees the vote to male citizens

1840   1850   1860   1870

1881: Marshall Field renames his Chicago, Illinois, department store after himself.

J. L. Hudson opens his first department store in Detroit, Michigan.

1886: Atlanta pharmacist John Pemberton invents the Coca-Cola formula.

David H. McConnell starts the California Perfume Company (later Avon) in New York.

1888: The first successful Kodak camera appears on the market.

1892: General Electric is formed through the merger of Thomas Edison's Edison General Electric and Thomson-Houston.

1894: Candy maker Milton Hershey sells his first milk chocolate bars.

1897: Olds Motor Vehicle Company is started by Ransom E. Olds.

1898: Caleb Bradham invents Pepsi-Cola.

1899: S. S. Kresge establishes the S. S. Kresge Company.

Bell changes his company name to American Telephone & Telegraph (AT&T).

1901: J. P. Morgan combines ten separate companies, including Carnegie Steel, to form the United States Steel Corporation.

1903: Ford Motor Company is founded.

David B. Buick founds the Buick Motor Company.

The Warner brothers show their first film at their home in Youngstown, Ohio.

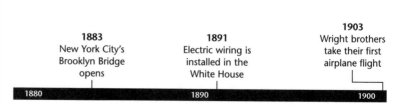

1883
New York City's
Brooklyn Bridge
opens

1891
Electric wiring is
installed in the
White House

1903
Wright brothers
take their first
airplane flight

1880   1890   1900

George Draper Dayton takes control of a Minneapolis dry-goods store and renames it Dayton's.

1906: W. K. Kellogg starts the Battle Creek Toasted Corn Flake Company.

1908: The Ford Model T is introduced.

General Motors Corporation is formed, incorporating the Buick Motor Company and the Olds Motor Vehicle Company.

1910: Joyce C. Hall starts a wholesale postcard business in Kansas City, Missouri.

1911: The Supreme Court orders the breakup of Standard Oil.

1912: L. L. Bean is formed in Freeport, Maine.

1913: Ford introduces the assembly line.

1917: William Boeing renames his aviation company The Boeing Airplane Company.

1919: Along with Westinghouse and other companies, General Electric forms the Radio Corporation of America (RCA).

1920: Eddie Bauer's Tennis Shop opens; name soon changes to Eddie Bauer's Sports Shop.

1922: Henry Luce forms Time, Inc.

1923: With his brother Roy, Walt Disney forms Disney Brothers Studio, which later becomes the Walt Disney Company.

1925: The Chrysler Corporation is formed from the Maxwell Motor Company.

1926: The National Broadcasting Company (NBC) is formed, with General Electric a part owner.

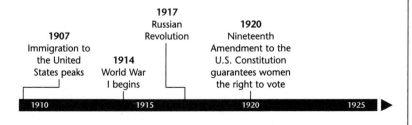

1928: Chrysler launches the Plymouth and DeSoto lines of automobiles.

1935: The first DC-3 airplane flight occurs on December 17.

1936: The United Auto Workers stage their first sit-down strike.

1938: Earl Tupper forms the Earl S. Tupper Company (later Tupperware, Inc.) to create industrial plastics.

1939: David Packard and William Hewlett form Hewlett-Packard to sell the audio oscillator they invented.

1942: All Chrysler, Ford, and General Motors plants convert to military production.

1947: Three Bell Labs scientists invent the transistor.

1948: Richard and Maurice McDonald open their first fast-food restaurant in San Bernadino, California.

Earl Tupper meets Brownie Wise, a sales representative for Stanley Home Products, who launches the concept of the Tupperware party.

1957: The first Japanese car, a Toyota, is sold in the United States.

1958: Bank of America launches the first credit card.

Bell Labs scientists invent the laser.

1959: Berry Gordy launches the Tamla and Motown record labels after borrowing $800 from his family.

1961: Ray Kroc takes full control of the McDonald's Corporation from the McDonald brothers.

1962: The first Wal-Mart store opens in Rogers, Arkansas.

The first Kmart store opens in a suburb of Detroit, Michigan.

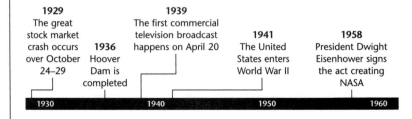

1929
The great stock market crash occurs over October 24–29

1936
Hoover Dam is completed

1939
The first commercial television broadcast happens on April 20

1941
The United States enters World War II

1958
President Dwight Eisenhower signs the act creating NASA

1930   1940   1950   1960

The Instamatic, Kodak's most popular camera ever, appears in stores.

The Coca-Cola Company introduces TAB diet cola.

1965: Ralph Nader publishes *Unsafe at Any Speed,* critical of General Motors and its Corvair.

1968: Blue Ribbon Sports's (later renamed Nike) first best-selling shoe, the Cortez, takes the United States by storm.

1969: Donald and Doris Fisher open the first Gap store in San Francisco, California.

Children's Television Workshop broadcasts the first episode of *Sesame Street.*

The J. L. Hudson Company and the Dayton Company merge to form the Dayton Hudson Corporation.

1971: The first Starbucks coffee shop opens in Seattle, Washington.

1973: From its hub airport in Memphis, Tennessee, FedEx begins service to twenty-five U.S. citites.

1974: Wally "Famous" Amos begins baking cookies to sell commercially.

1975: Bill Gates and Paul Allen form Microsoft to develop software for personal computers.

1976: Steve Jobs and Steve Wozniak form the Apple Computer Company and sell their first personal computers.

Former model and stockbroker Martha Stewart starts a catering business in her Westport, Connecticut, home.

1978: Ben Cohen and Jerry Greenfield start Ben & Jerry's Homemade Inc., and open their first ice cream scoop shop in Burlington, Vermont.

Lee Iacocca becomes the head Chrysler.

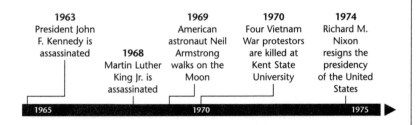

| 1963 President John F. Kennedy is assassinated | 1968 Martin Luther King Jr. is assassinated | 1969 American astronaut Neil Armstrong walks on the Moon | 1970 Four Vietnam War protestors are killed at Kent State University | 1974 Richard M. Nixon resigns the presidency of the United States |

1965 · · · · · · · · · · 1970 · · · · · · · · · · 1975 ▶

Toys R Us revives the employee stock option as an employee benefit.

1979: Bernie Marcus and Arthur Blank open the first three Home Depot stores in Atlanta, Georgia.

1980: Ted Turner starts CNN, the first twenty-four-hour cable news station.

1981: IBM sells the first personal computer using the Microsoft Disk Operating System (MS-DOS).

1984: Apple introduces the Macintosh computer, which includes such features as a mouse and graphical user interface.

AT&T is divided up into seven regional phone companies.

Michael Dell officially forms Dell Computer Corporation; Dell becomes one of the first companies to make clones of IBM personal computers.

1985: Steve Case helps start Quantum Computer Services, which later becomes America Online (AOL).

The Ben & Jerry's Foundation is established, funded by 7.5 percent of the company's annual profits before taxes, to give to community-oriented nonprofit groups.

A.M. Chicago becomes *The Oprah Winfrey Show;* the following year Winfrey forms Harpo Productions, Inc.

Nike signs basketball great Michael Jordan to promote its shoes.

1987: Microsoft Bookshelf is Microsoft's first product on CD-ROM.

1989: Time, Inc., and Warner Communications merge, forming Time Warner.

1981 Sandra Day O'Connor becomes the first female U.S. Supreme Court justice	**1986** The space shuttle *Challenger* explodes	**1987** The Black Monday stock market crash threatens the American economy	**1989** The Berlin Wall is torn down
1980	1985		1990

1990: Dayton Hudson Corporation buys Marshall Field's.

Vera Wang Bridal House Ltd. opens on Madison Avenue in New York.

1994: Jeffrey Katzenberg, Steven Spielberg, and David Geffen join forces to form a new entertainment company, DreamWorks SKG.

General Electric launches www.ge.com, becoming the first Fortune 500 company to go online.

Mosaic Communications Corporation is founded by Marc Andreessen and James Clark; named changes to Netscape Communications Corporation.

1995: Jeff Bezos opens Amazon.com on the Internet, offering one million titles.

Netscape offers its stock to the public on the stock market.

1996: AT&T splits again into three companies and Lucent Technologies is born.

Time Warner buys Turner Broadcasting System.

Microsoft and General Electric (owner of NBC) launch computer/television network MSNBC.

1997: The Boeing Company merges with McDonnell Douglas.

Martha Stewart buys her magazine *Martha Stewart Living* from Time Warner and launches Martha Stewart Living Omnimedia, Inc.

1998: The U.S. Justice Department accuses Microsoft of violating antitrust laws.

Chrysler merges with Daimler-Benz to become Daimler-Chrysler AG.

1999: Netscape is bought by America Online for $4.2 billion.

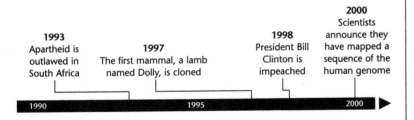

1993
Apartheid is
outlawed in
South Africa

1997
The first mammal, a lamb
named Dolly, is cloned

1998
President Bill
Clinton is
impeached

2000
Scientists
announce they
have mapped a
sequence of the
human genome

1990   1995   2000

2000: Reflecting the growth of its discount stores, Dayton Hudson changes its name to Target Corporation.

The British-Dutch conglomerate Unilever buys Ben & Jerry's for $236 million and vows it will maintain the Vermont company's social and environmental commitments.

Children's Television Workshop changes its name to Sesame Workshop.

2001: Amazon.com posts its first profit, $5.1 million in the fourth quarter.

America Online purchases Time Warner, forming AOL Time Warner.

2002: Kmart Corporation files for Chapter 11 bankruptcy protection.

The purchase of Compaq Computer Corporation makes Hewlett-Packard the second-largest computer manufacturer in the world.

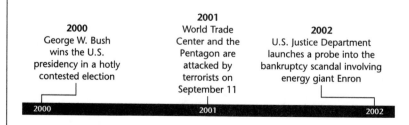

2000
George W. Bush wins the U.S. presidency in a hotly contested election

2001
World Trade Center and the Pentagon are attacked by terrorists on September 11

2002
U.S. Justice Department launches a probe into the bankruptcy scandal involving energy giant Enron

2000   2001   2002

Leading American Businesses

Profiles of Major American Companies
and the People Who Made Them Important

Gap, Inc.

1 Harrison Street
San Francisco, CA 94105
(650) 427-2000
www.gapinc.com

Since the 1950s, many U.S. companies have made money targeting baby boomers, the generation born between 1946 and 1964. Tailoring products to the tastes of these seventy-six million Americans—and later, their children—helped Gap, Inc., become the largest clothing-store chain in the United States. What started as a single San Francisco shop has grown into a retailing giant with more than four thousand stores around the world. The Gap's casual, well-made clothes—especially khakis, jeans, and T-shirts—have become part of American fashion, worn by people of all ages and from all economic backgrounds.

Falling into the Gap

The first Gap store was established because founder Donald Fisher had trouble finding blue jeans in his size. Although he had no experience in retail, he and his wife Doris decided to open a clothing store in San Francisco, California, that would feature Levi's jeans in a wide range of sizes. The couple also sold records in their store, which they named the Gap, a reference to the so-called "generation gap" between

Gap at a Glance

- **Employees:** 166,000

- **CEO:** Millard "Mickey" Drexler

- **Subsidiaries:** Banana Republic Companies; GPS Companies; GPSDC, Inc.; Gap Companies; Goldhawk B.V.; Melanie Rennes Saint Germain SARL; Old Navy Companies; Real Estate Ventures

- **Major Competitors:** TJX Companies, Inc.; American Eagle Outfitters; Intimate Brands, Inc.; Abercrombie & Fitch; Limited, Inc.

- **Notable Stores:** GapKids; babyGap; GapBody; Banana Republic; Old Navy

young people and adults. The store was meant to attract college students and teenagers. The first Gap opened in August 1969 near San Francisco State College, and ads promised that customers would find "four tons" of Levi's jeans for sale. In 1992, Fisher told *Business Week* that the first Gap did so well, "you couldn't get into the store."

After his early success, Fisher stopped selling records and concentrated on jeans, while adding other casual clothes to his inventory. The Gap grew, opening more stores in California, and then in other states. In 1974, the company began producing its own clothes. Denim, however, remained the company's major product, and Levi's was the top brand. Radio and television ads encouraged shoppers to "Fall into the Gap" for affordable, fashionable clothes. By 1976, the Gap had two hundred stores across the United States.

But even as the Gap grew, the company faced some problems. For years, Levi's had not allowed retailers to offer sales on its jeans—stores had to charge what **Levi Strauss & Company** (see entry) told them to charge. In 1976, however, the Federal Trade Commission (FTC) ruled that manufacturers could not order stores to charge a minimum price. As other stores slashed prices on Levi's, the Gap saw profits fall. And in the early 1980s, the demand for denim clothes began to slow. Fisher needed to make changes to keep the Gap growing.

New Stores, New Leader

In 1982, Fisher began expanding the size of the typical Gap store, making it up to three times larger. With the extra space, the stores carried a wider range of clothes. The next year, the Gap bought the Banana Republic, a clothing retailer with two stores in San Francisco and a mail-order business. The stores

Timeline

1969: Donald and Doris Fisher open the first Gap store in San Francisco, California.

1974: The Gap begins designing and selling its own clothes.

1983: Fisher buys the Banana Republic and hires Mickey Drexler to run the Gap stores.

1984: The Gap stops selling all brand-name clothes except Levi's.

1986: First GapKids store opens.

1987: First international Gap store opens in London.

1990: babyGap brand is introduced at GapKids.

1991: The Gap stops carrying Levi's and sells only its own Gap brand of clothes.

1994: Old Navy opens its first stores.

1995: Mickey Drexler becomes CEO of Gap, Inc.

2002: Gap announces that Mickey Drexler will be retiring at the end of the year.

had an African safari theme and featured clothes made from khaki, a light-brown cotton cloth often used for military uniforms. Fisher soon built more Banana Republic stores and sales grew almost 500 percent between 1985 and 1987.

Fisher's best move was bringing in a clothing retail expert to help him run the company. Millard "Mickey" Drexler had boosted sales at Ann Taylor, a chain of women's dress stores. Fisher named him president of the Gap stores and let him go to work. Drexler began by slashing prices to sell off old merchandise, so he could introduce new clothes. Both profits and the company's stock price plunged, and Drexler later told *Business Week,* "We were all scared, and I was more scared than anyone the first year and a half."

But as Drexler implemented his ideas, the Gap began to rebound. To Drexler, the store's old lines were "trendy but not tasteful," as he told the *New York Times* in 1991. Realizing that the long-time Gap customers—baby boomers—were getting older and wanted more style, Drexler switched to better

The initial success of Banana Republic was often linked to the popularity of several 1980s movies, *Raiders of the Lost Ark, Romancing the Stone,* and *Out of Africa,* which featured exotic locations and stars wearing khaki and other outdoor clothing. By 1988, the fad for "safari" styles ended, and Banana Republic struggled. The Gap restructured the stores, getting rid of tropical decorations and offering sportswear for men and women. Today, Banana Republic targets customers willing to pay more than the typical Gap shopper.

fabrics and classic designs, offering items in many colors. He also got rid of all the brand-name clothes except Levi's. (The Gap stopped selling Levi's in 1991.) Everything else in the stores was designed by the company and bore the "Gap" label. Drexler made changes within the stores, too, displaying clothes on white shelves instead of hanging them from metal racks. Store walls were painted white, and the wood floors were polished twice a week to give the spaces a fresh, clean look. The new Gap attracted both adults and young people, and by 1986, sales had risen 40 percent from 1983.

Expanding the Market

In 1986, Drexler saw another need the Gap could fill: providing durable clothes for children. The company launched GapKids, separate stores targeted to children between ages three and twelve. Parents quickly responded, and the new division's annual sales reached $260 million in 1991. By then, the stores were also selling babyGap clothes, designed for infants and toddlers. Today, the Gap has separate stores for its line of kiddy apparel. In 1990, Drexler told *Fortune* magazine, "I didn't know if GapKids was going to work.... I do know you can't run a business without taking risks."

Helping the Gap grow was the company's advertising. In 1988, a series of black-and-white magazine ads featured celebrities wearing Gap clothing along with other items from their wardrobe. Called "Individuals of Style," the campaign's message was that Gap clothes were for everyone and they went with everything. Some of the ads featured Gap T-shirts, and sales of these simple tops soared. A later advertising campaign showed celebrities from the past, such as Marilyn Monroe (1926–1962), wearing khakis, sparking new popularity for the pants.

In 1994, Gap, Inc., added another new division, Old Navy. With larger stores than the typical Gap, Old Navy car-

ried clothes for the entire family, selling them at lower prices than the Gap. Trying to create a fun atmosphere, the company decorated the stores playfully, sometimes including old cars and gumball machines. In less than four years, Old Navy reached annual sales of $1 billion. By this time, the Gap had also expanded overseas, introducing stores in Canada and Europe. The first Japanese store opened in 1995. New products were also introduced, as the Gap began selling shoes and perfume.

The Gap started out selling just blue jeans, but has moved on to become a large seller of business casual clothes.
Reproduced by permission of the Fashion Syndicate Press.

Difficult Times

During the 1990s, the Gap and its other retail divisions grew dramatically. The company also began offering its products on-line, through several different Web sites. Although sales increased each year, the company started having some troubles in 2000. The boost in sales came from adding new stores, not from selling more clothes at existing stores. The Gap tried

Fighting "Sweatshops"

Although the Gap boomed during the 1990s, the company heard growing criticism about some of its business practices. Social reformers attacked the Gap, along with other clothing companies, for the conditions in some of the overseas factories where their clothing was made. The factories were called "sweatshops," where workers, usually young women, worked long hours for low wages. The protests centered on the Pacific island of Saipan, a U.S. territory. In response, the Gap established its Code of Vendor Conduct. The company pledged to check working conditions in the factories and not hire manufacturers that did not meet minimum standards for wages and safety. On its Web site, however, the company acknowledged that "People shouldn't assume that because we have a Code the garment manufacturers that get our business are in 100 percent compliance." Protesters still target the Gap, while the company continues to strengthen its code.

adding clothes meant to attract younger shoppers, but the new styles did not appeal to older customers. In 2001, Drexler admitted to *Fortune*, "We have disappointed some of our core customers."

To combat its slump, the Gap planned to slow its expansion and concentrate on winning back those old customers. While still concentrating on such basics as denim, Drexler added new fashions, hoping to find the right mix. Despite tough times, Drexler remained confident in the company's future. "At the end of the day" he told *Fortune*, "Gap is a very, very well-respected, popular, and recognized brand."

Donald Fisher

Born: 1928
San Francisco, California
Founder and chairman of the board, Gap, Inc.

For the Gap's Donald Fisher, a key concept has always been "value." The company's definition of that word has changed over the years. When the Gap first opened in 1969, value meant a wide variety of blue jeans, particularly Levi's, in one store. Later, value meant low prices for casual clothes. Finally, in their most successful years, Fisher and the Gap defined value as well-made, stylish clothes at reasonable prices. In 1991, Fisher told a group of apparel manufacturers that his company was dedicated to providing "what the consumers want, when they want it."

Unexpected Career

Donald George Fisher was born in 1928 in San Francisco, California. Both his father and grandfather developed real estate in the city, and Fisher followed them into that business. First, however, he attended the University of California, Berkeley, where he graduated in 1950 after studying business and finance. In college, he was an All-American swimmer and star water-polo player. After college, Fisher worked with his father

"You could have a great high-priced garment that's the best quality in the world and still be offering great value to the customer. You could have something that's very cheap and made out of terrible quality fabric and you wouldn't be offering value to the customer. I think what we've done is married the price ... and the quality."

An avid art collector, Donald Fisher hung some of his purchases at the Gap's San Francisco headquarters. These included works by such twentieth-century American masters as Alexander Calder (1898–1976) and Roy Liechtenstein (1923–1997).

in real estate, then served as president of the Fisher Property Investment Company. He also married Doris Feigenbaum, with whom he eventually had three sons, Robert, William, and John.

Fisher raised his family in his hometown, where he developed property. Although not a particularly tall man, Fisher had trouble in San Francisco finding blue jeans long enough to fit his thirty-four-inch legs. He and his wife decided to invest $100,000 to open their own store dedicated to jeans, and the Gap was born in 1969. The company grew quickly, opening two hundred stores in several years. It also took on the added responsibility of designing its own clothes. By some accounts, offering these "private label" brands, with such names as Foxtails and Durango, helped the Gap survive some difficult years in the late 1970s. By 1983, the Gap had more than five hundred stores, and Fisher added a new division, Banana Republic.

Despite his success, Fisher was considered better at finding locations for the stores and building them than he was at running a clothing business. By the early 1980s, the company was struggling, and Fisher talked to several retail experts about how to spark new growth. In 1983, he hired Millard "Mickey" Drexler to run day-to-day operations for the Gap stores, while Fisher focused on Banana Republic and the corporation's overall operations. Drexler, Fisher later told *Fortune,* was the only person he found who could execute his vision. "I wanted to be different," Fisher said, "I wanted to cut out the middleman."

Changing Roles

Although Fisher was chairman and chief executive officer (CEO) of Gap, Inc., he eventually gave Drexler more freedom to run the entire company. In 1987, an unnamed retail expert told *Fortune,* "It takes a very special chairman to put his ego behind him and let a hero come in and take over." Fisher, however, had shown this kind of modesty throughout his life. Even as his wealth grew, Fisher stayed in the same home he

Mickey Drexler: The Casual Leader

"I find clothing very complicated to buy. It shouldn't be that complicated. It should be simple," Gap chief executive office (CEO) Mickey Drexler said in a 1998 interview with *Fortune*. At the Gap, Drexler brought simplicity to his customers by offering just one brand and sticking to such basics as blue jeans, khakis, and T-shirts. Drexler is a simple man himself, preferring to wear casual clothes to work. And like his boss, Donald Fisher, Drexler avoids publicity. His focus has always been on the Gap and helping it grow.

Millard "Mickey" Drexler was born on August 17, 1944, in New York City. Always interested in business, he spent his summers during college working for a department store chain. After earning a master's of business administration (MBA) degree at Boston University, Drexler took a job at Bloomingdale's, a fashionable New York store. After jobs at several other stores, Drexler was named president at Ann Taylor, which sells women's clothing. The company was struggling at the time, but Drexler quickly turned it around.

With his success at Ann Taylor, Drexler caught the attention of the Gap's Fisher. Drexler's changes at the Gap turned it into a retail-clothing giant. Drexler took charge of deciding what clothes to sell, and he often visited the stores to ask salespeople what customers liked. Working on hunches, not market research, Drexler proposed the GapKids line when he had trouble finding good clothes for his own son. In 1994, Drexler saw the rise of discount stores and opened Old Navy, the Gap's division for budget clothes. In 1995, Fisher rewarded Drexler by naming him president and CEO of the Gap. Fisher said in a press statement, "Due largely to his efforts, The Gap … has become one of the most recognizable consumer names in the world."

By 2000, however, the Gap had lost some ground to competitors, and some business analysts blamed Drexler. People began to say he was too involved in every detail of the company and too easily changed his mind. Still, Drexler kept the confidence of the Gap's board of directors. One of them, **Apple Computer, Inc.** (see entry) president **Steve Jobs**, said in *Business Week* that Drexler was a creative person: "he's not a robot—he's a human being with moods. When he sees something he doesn't like, he says so."

had built in the 1950s, and he was known to ask for tap water while making business deals in restaurants.

Although Drexler chose the merchandise and perfected the design of the stores, Fisher remained active on the manufacturing end. He dealt with clothing manufacturers from around the world and pushed the use of computers so designers in New York could easily share ideas with the corporate offices in San Francisco. He and Drexler also worked hard to keep the company's debt low. The company's growth also gave the Gap an advantage over its competition. In 1992, Fisher told *California Business*, "We do have the ability to buy things at better prices because of our size.... There's nobody that's in every mall, doing what we do."

In 1995, Fisher stepped down as CEO of the Gap, keeping only the title of chairman. Drexler then took charge of the entire corporation. By then, the Fishers were billionaires, and the Gap's founder was already spending more time with interests outside the company. An active Republican, Fisher had served on a U.S. government advisory council on international trade since the 1980s, and he contributed money to many political candidates. During the 1990s, Fisher remained active in real estate, using some of his Gap profits to buy hotels and bid on developments in San Francisco. In the city, he helped start the San Francisco Partnership, to promote business growth there. Fisher and his family also bought 235,000 acres of California timberland.

In addition, Fisher was involved in public service, serving on the board of trustees at Princeton University, where his sons went to school. In 2001, he was appointed to the California State Board of Education. He had shown an earlier interest in public education in San Francisco. In 1998, Fisher convinced city officials to hire the Edison Corporation of New York to run a local elementary school. Fisher also donated millions of dollars to schools run by Edison, a private company. Fisher's ties to Edison were criticized because his son John was an investor in the company. Fisher's charitable foundation also received favorable prices on Edison stock. Despite those concerns, a California education official praised Fisher's appointment to the state board of education. In the *San Francisco Chronicle*, Diana Michel said Fisher had "strong ties to business and a really good understanding of the most recent changes at the state level in terms of bringing standards to schools."

Some of Fisher's other activities have also drawn criticism. Environmentalists have attacked the Fisher family's cutting of redwood trees on its timberlands. In San Francisco, critics say Fisher has used his wealth to unfairly influence city politics, leading to favorable deals for the Gap. According to a 1998 report in the *San Francisco Bay Guardian,* Fisher's influence led the city to sell a prime piece of land along the waterfront to the Gap at an incredibly low price. Fisher has also been the target of protests because of the Gap's ties to foreign factories referred to as "sweatshops."

Despite these criticisms, Fisher won the respect of politicians and business leaders for his success at the Gap, and the vision he showed in picking Drexler to rejuvenate the company during its difficult times.

For More Information

Periodicals

Asimov, Nanette. "Business Influence for State's Schools." *San Francisco Chronicle* (March 16, 1991).

Creswell, Julie. "Confessions of a Fashion Victim: Gap." *Fortune* (December 10, 2001): p. 48.

"Donald Fisher." *California Business* (May 1992): p. 23.

"Gap: Missing That Ol' Mickey Magic." *Business Week* (October 29, 2001): p. 86.

Larson, Kristin. "Curing What Ails the Gap." *Women's Wear Daily* (October 2, 2001): p. 72.

Mitchell, Russell. "The Gap." *Business Week* (March 9, 1992).

Munk, Nina. "Gap Gets It." *Fortune* (August 3, 1998): p. 68.

Palmieri, Jean. "Drexler Getting CEO Post at Gap; Fisher to Remain as Chairman." *Daily News Record* (September 13, 1995): p. 1.

Smith, Sarah. "The Billionaires: The Supermen of Specialty Stores." *Fortune* (October 12, 1987): p. 142.

"Sweatshop Watch." [On-line] http://www.sweatshopwatch.org (accessed on August 15, 2002).

Zoll, Daniel. "The Fisher King." *San Francisco Bay Guardian* (August 12, 1998).

Web Sites

Gap, Inc. [On-line] http://www.gapinc.com (accessed on August 15, 2002).

General Electric, Inc.

3135 Easton Turnpike
Fairfield, CT 06431
(203) 373-2211
www.ge.com

From the beginning, General Electric (GE) was a leader among U.S. companies. It dominated the lighting industry, played an important role in the development of broadcasting, and contributed significant scientific inventions that led to many of the consumer and industrial products used today. The company realized early the importance of technological innovation and pioneered the idea of corporations operating their own research labs.

General Electric was also a leader in management techniques. Many U.S. and later international companies followed the principles introduced by GE, from strategic planning to doing business on-line. Even the company's leaders were well known, making an impact both on other businesses and on the U.S. government.

A Focus on Research

General Electric was formed in 1892 through the merger of Edison General Electric, a company that managed the many businesses and inventions of Thomas Edison

(1847–1931), and Thomson-Houston, which held several patents in the growing field of electricity. Charles Coffin became the first president of General Electric, which employed ten thousand people. His first objective was to keep the company in business during a depression that occurred in 1893 and caused many firms in the electrical industry to fold.

From the beginning, Coffin realized that GE needed to use technology to answer consumer needs. As competing companies increasingly began to catch up to GE with new lighting and other electric products, GE opened the first industrial research laboratory. The purpose of the lab, which opened in 1900, was to do research that would allow GE to develop or improve products for sale to the public. The lab was headed by Charles Proteus Steinmetz (1865–1923), a strong supporter of the idea that research and development should be done within a company, rather than relying on outside scientists. Steinmetz made many discoveries and was later referred to as "the Wizard of Electricity."

General Electric at a Glance

- **Employees:** 313,000

- **CEO:** Jeffrey R. Immelt

- **Subsidiaries:** CFN International; GE Aircraft Engines; GE Appliances; GE Equity; GE Financial Assurance Holdings; GE Lighting; GE Medical Systems; GE Plastics; Heller Financial, Inc.; National Broadcasting Company, Inc.

- **Major Competitors:** ALSTOM; CIT Group; Siemens

- **Notable Products and Services:** Hotpoint appliances; GE light bulbs, electronics, and industrial products; RCA electronics; Television networks: NBC, CNBC, MSNBC

Some of GE's early products included X-ray machines and steam turbines, as well as components that helped advance such areas as medicine and train transportation. The company was especially active in producing consumer products, the first of which was the Hotpoint iron. In 1910, GE introduced its Hotpoint electric range, which became one of its flagship items. Other appliances followed, including the Monitor Top refrigerator in 1927. Before this, only a few thousand families in the United States had refrigerators and only about half had iceboxes, boxes that used purchased ice to keep food fresh. During the 1930s, GE introduced many helpful household appliances, including electric washing machines, air conditioners, and the garbage disposal unit.

Timeline

1892: General Electric is formed through the merger of Thomas Edison's Edison General Electric and Thomson-Houston.

1900: GE opens the first industrial research laboratory.

1910: GE introduces the Hotpoint electric range.

1919: Along with Westinghouse and other companies, GE forms the Radio Corporation of America (RCA).

1922: GE launches one of the first radio stations, WGY in Schenectady, New York.

1926: NBC is formed, with GE a part owner.

1932: Under pressure from the government, GE sells its ownership share in RCA.

1939: GE scientist Katherine Burr Blodgett invents invisible glass, which becomes the basis for today's camera lenses.

1941: GE's TV station WRGB is credited with being the first television network, along with a station in New York.

1941: GE builds the nation's first jet engine, the 1-A.

1962: GE scientist Bob Hall develops the laser.

1981: New CEO Jack Welch lays off 25 percent of the company's workforce.

1986: GE buys RCA and its flagship NBC.

1994: GE becomes the first Fortune 500 company to go on-line.

1996: Microsoft Corporation and GE launch computer/television network MSNBC.

2001: GE's best-known leader, Jack Welch, retires.

An Important Role in Broadcasting

General Electric was also instrumental in the development of radio and later television broadcasting. Not only did it manufacture parts that allowed sound to be broadcast over radio waves, but in 1922 it started radio station WGY in Schenectady, New York, one of the first stations in the country.

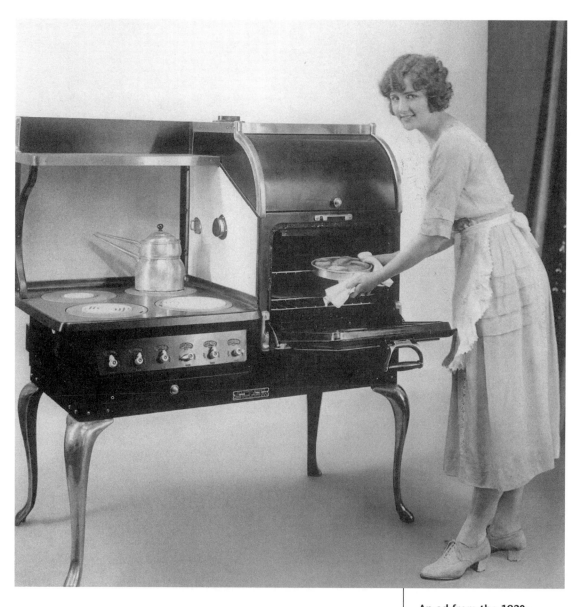

In 1919, GE helped form the Radio Corporation of America (RCA) and became a part owner, with several other companies, of the first radio network, the National Broadcasting Company (NBC). Although a federal court ordered GE to sell its share in RCA in 1932, it continued to be active in broadcasting. In 1941, the television station WRGB, also in Schenectady and owned by GE, became the first station to receive

Katherine Burr Blodgett (1898–1979) was the first woman scientist at the GE Research Laboratory. She is best known for her invention of invisible glass, a coated, non-reflecting glass, in 1939. Her discovery directly led to the materials that are used today in almost all camera lenses and other optic lenses.

television broadcasts from New York, representing the first television network.

Technology through the Decades

GE developed many industrial products throughout the 1940s. It built the United States's first jet engine, called the 1-A, in 1941, and oversaw the first commercial use of radar to assist ship and submarine navigation. Company scientist Vincent Schaefer developed cloud seeding—the process of making rain—which is used in farming to protect fields from hail.

GE's innovations continued into the 1950s, when it developed all-weather headlamps for automobiles, allowing drivers to see better, and created a process for making artificial diamonds, which are used in industry for cutting and smoothing. In the 1960s, GE was instrumental in making parts for the U.S. space program. In 1962, scientist Bob Hall developed the laser, which eventually made the CD player and laser printer possible.

In the 1970s, GE introduced the first digital clock radio that could be programmed, while inventing a stream of products for medical and industrial use. In 1978, GE Lighting produced the material necessary to make the first fiber optic strands. This was the beginning of a revolution in communications that enabled data to travel much faster than ever before.

Always the innovator, GE became the first large corporation (the first in the Fortune 500) to go on-line, with the exception of firms in the computer industry. It launched its Web site, www.ge.com, in 1994. In 1996, it integrated television with the Internet when it introduced MSNBC, a joint venture between its subsidiary NBC and the **Microsoft Corporation** (see entry) that allowed viewers to get their news and information either on cable television or over the web.

Innovation in Management

Meanwhile, GE was also becoming known for its progressive management techniques and talented executives.

Throughout the company's history, which spans over one hundred years, there were only twelve CEOs (the last was named in 2001). This is fairly amazing considering that many large corporations are constantly changing management. Almost all of General Electric's CEOs have became well known in business and government circles, and many of them wrote books about their business philosophies.

In the 1920s and 1930s, GE pioneered what was called "enlightened management" ideas, such as giving workers paid vacations. Later, in the 1950s, the company's fifth CEO, Ralph I. Cordiner, refined the concept of decentralization—which had been used in some industries since World War I (1914–18)—by making 120 GE departments into separate profitable centers. Each general manager was responsible for the performance of his or her unit. That structure led to more layers of management and increased employee fear—workers thought they might lose their jobs if their unit was not successful. The system, however, worked for the overall benefit of the company during this period.

Tom Brokaw, anchor the the *NBC Nightly News.* **General Electric owns NBC along with a variety of other businesses.**
Reproduced by permission of AP/Wide World Photos.

In the 1960s, GE invested a lot of money in new businesses as it continued to expand. Rather than deciding in a systematic way which businesses to go into, it put money into many industries and waited to see which would end up being profitable. Some did well, but the company became hard to manage. And, in spite of the movement into new businesses, 80 percent of the company's profits still came from its original interest, electrical products and equipment.

GE became one of the first companies to support the concept of strategic planning during the 1970s. In strategic planning, executives analyze industries so they can identify those where the company is strongest. Reginald Jones, who headed the company in the 1970s, supported the idea that government

NBC: The Nation's First Broadcast Network

The Radio Corporation of America (RCA) was formed in 1919 by General Electric, Westinghouse Electric, AT&T, and United Fruit. All of these companies had a keen interest in a brand new "wireless" industry known as radio. From the beginning, RCA was a leader in radio, both manufacturing radios and controlling the two largest radio networks in the United States. The networks were part of the National Broadcasting Corporation (NBC), RCA's subsidiary.

NBC was formed in 1926 when RCA purchased AT&T's radio stations, including the main station, WEAF in New York. RCA owned 50 percent of NBC, while GE claimed 30 percent and Westinghouse 20 percent.

NBC was divided into two networks, the Red and the Blue. The Red network was more entertainment and commercially oriented, while the Blue focused on public service. Together, the networks consisted of nineteen stations in 1926. Ten years later they had grown to one hundred stations.

In 1936, the government forced RCA and its leader David Sarnoff (1891–1971; a pioneer in both radio and television) to sell off its Blue network—which became the American Broadcasting Corporation (ABC)—in order to increase competition in radio broadcasting. The Red network continued to operate under the NBC name. Four years earlier, GE and Westinghouse had been ordered

and business should work together. He served as an adviser to three U.S. presidents. *U.S. News & World Report* said at the time that Jones was viewed by his fellow executives as "the most influential person in business."

The Welch Years and Beyond

Jones was followed as chairman and CEO by Jack Welch, who became one of the best-known and admired, although controversial, business executives in the world. He strengthened GE's performance, first by cutting 25 percent of the workforce and eliminating weak businesses, then by acquiring stronger companies. Between 1981 and 1985 alone, he purchased three hundred companies. He also cut out unnecessary levels of management and placed some of the decision-making power with the workers. He retired in 2001, replaced by Jeffrey R. Immelt.

to sell off their interests in RCA, also for competitive reasons.

While radio was growing quickly, RCA was also working on a new technology, television broadcasting. The first image broadcast over television was a figurine of the cartoon character Felix the Cat rotating on a turntable.

Television caught on slowly at first. By 1947 only eight thousand homes in the United States had television sets, which were very expensive at the time. Sarnoff decided to broadcast the 1947 World Series between the New York Yankees and Brooklyn Dodgers to drum up interest for TV. The broadcast was blurry and hard to follow, but the series was hard-fought and exciting and it encouraged many people who had seen it on television in bars and restaurants to purchase a television set for their homes. By 1948 there were three hundred thousand sets in the United States and four million by 1950.

The NBC of the 2000s, still a subsidiary of RCA (which GE purchased in 1986), included many different interests, including fourteen stations, the NBC television network, the Spanish-language network Telemundo, cable network CNBC, and cable/Internet network MSNBC, a joint venture with the **Microsoft Corporation** (see entry). NBC also had an interest in the PAX Network and produced and distributed its own television programming in news, entertainment, and sports.

Welch purchased some big companies during his leadership of GE. He bought RCA, for example, which GE had partially owned in the early half of the twentieth century. GE moved into the investment field, bought electrical lighting firms in emerging countries (such as those in Eastern Europe), and added companies in the chemical field. Not all of these were a perfect fit, but they contributed to GE's growth in the 1980s and 1990s.

In one notable setback, GE tried to acquire Honeywell International in 2001 but was prevented from doing so by the government of the European Union. That same year, the company was ordered to remove cancer-causing chemicals called PCBs from the Hudson River in New York. A court found it had dumped the harmful chemicals there over several years and ordered the company to clean up the river at a cost of $460 million.

Despite these stumbles, GE's stock price went up by 3,000 percent during Welch's time as CEO. His successes continued General Electric's more than one-hundred-year history of proven performance and business leadership.

Jack Welch

Born: November 19, 1935
Peabody, Massachusetts
Former CEO, General Electric, Inc.

Jack Welch.
Reproduced by permission of Archive Photos, Inc.

During Jack Welch's twenty years as the leader of General Electric, he became one of the best-known business leaders in the world. He made GE more profitable and more valuable by making its management structure less complicated and by focusing on the businesses where the company was most efficient. Some of his methods attracted a lot of criticism. But there are few corporate leaders who have received as much publicity or as much admiration as Jack Welch.

"Dealing with the best team wins. This whole idea—whether it's a hockey team, a baseball team or a business—is the same: if you have the best team, you win."

Climbing the GE Ladder

John Francis Welch Jr., known as Jack, was born in 1935 in Peabody, Massachusetts. His father John worked for the Boston & Maine Railroad as a conductor and was often away from home because of his job. Jack's mother Grace was a strong force in the early life of her only child. She encouraged Jack to do many things on his own, such as go to baseball games in the city alone, in order to make him independent. She also made him realize he could succeed in life, in spite of the fact that he spoke with a stutter and was one of the smallest kids in his

Jeffrey R. Immelt, the man who eventually replaced Jack Welch as CEO of General Electric in 2001, told *People* magazine that working for Welch could be "fun" or it could be "terrifying."

neighborhood. She always stressed the importance of education.

After graduating from high school, where he played four sports, Welch went to the University of Massachusetts at Amherst to study chemical engineering. He graduated in 1957 and went on to the University of Illinois for his masters and doctorate degrees. Immediately after he completed his studies in 1960, he took a job with General Electric, at a plant in Massachusetts. Managers there noticed he had an unusual combination of scientific knowledge and business sense. He also gained a reputation for rubbing people the wrong way at times, but his success at his job earned him the respect of his bosses.

Welch moved up quickly through GE, becoming general manager of the company's plastics division and turning it into one of the leading players in that industry. He became a vice president of General Electric in 1972 and moved to GE's consumer goods and services division in 1977. He became a vice chairman in 1979 and was assigned to the GE Credit Corporation. This was where he really made his mark. He got the division to grow by entering into new businesses; his results were soon noticed by top GE executives.

Neutron Jack

In 1981, Welch was named CEO and chairman of GE, becoming the youngest person ever to achieve this position at the company. He realized from the start that he needed to make some changes in order to stay competitive. He decided to reorganize the company by focusing only on those businesses that were strongest. During the course of this streamlining process, he laid off 135,000 GE employees—25 percent of the company's workers. By letting go of more than one hundred thousand workers after taking over the leadership of GE, Welch earned the nickname "Neutron Jack." The name comes from the neutron bomb, which wipes out all life but leaves buildings standing.

Businesses that were not ranked number one or number two in their industries were given an ultimatum to improve or be shut down. In the next five years, GE closed 73 plants and offices and sold 232 businesses. Meanwhile, all of GE's various companies were organized into three umbrella groups: manufacturing, services, and technology.

While Welch's early moves as CEO were controversial, people soon saw that his tactics made the company grow and become more efficient. Opinions of him began to improve. His reputation was also helped because he believed in placing some of the decision-making power with the workers on the factory floors, rather than leaving it all to management. This helped the company act on good ideas that managers might not have considered, and also improved the workers' morale.

At the same time that Welch was letting go of less profitable businesses, such as television sets and mining, he was buying companies in industries where he saw potential. Some of his purchases included the investment bank Kidder Peabody, the chemical company Borg-Warner, and RCA, the parent corporation of the television network NBC. The last deal, which cost $6.4 billion, was the largest merger outside the oil industry up to that time.

A Few Stumbles

Some of Welch's deals ending up causing headaches for Welch and for General Electric. When it was purchased NBC was the leader in television, but it started to lose ratings because of increased competition, especially from cable television networks. One of Kidder Peabody's top executives was put in jail for making deals based on information that was not public, known as "insider trading." Other scandals also occurred within the company during this period.

Many members of the press and competing corporate executives questioned Welch's decisions. For example, GE suffered a $120 million loss because Welch decided to move into the business of making automation equipment for factories, but then could not find enough customers to purchase the company's products. He also stayed out of some lucrative businesses that could have boosted company revenues. For example, he turned away from developing magnetic levitation (maglev), a new transportation technology, preferring to remain involved

At the time of Jack Welch's retirement in 2001, GE was the most valuable company in the world. Financial analysts estimated it was worth $490 billion. When Welch took over the company two decades earlier, the value was $14 billion.

in traditional railroad equipment, which was not a growing industry.

Despite these setbacks, Welch's reputation as an admired business leader grew. His methods of managing, which allowed employees to have a say in management decisions, were embraced by many other companies. Welch put company-wide quality initiatives in place and pushed GE to the Internet as a means to make the company more efficient. Probably the most significant factor in Welch's good reputation came from the fact that GE's value grew strongly throughout his twenty years as CEO.

At the end of Welch's career, he suffered a big business disappointment. He wanted to purchase Honeywell International, which made electronic equipment for airplanes. Its business fit well with GE's airplane-engine manufacturing operations. The two companies worked out the details for what would be history's largest industrial merger. The snag came when the newly formed European Union, the government that oversees matters affecting most of the countries in Europe, refused to grant permission for the merger. The EU required too many changes for GE and Honeywell to accept, so the deal fell apart.

The End of a Long Career

Welch retired from General Electric in 2001. His memoir, *Jack: Straight from the Gut,* which was one of many books Welch wrote over his career, became a best-seller as executives looked to his words of advice. Welch's personal reputation suffered in 2002, however, when an editor at the *Harvard Business Review,* Suzy Wetlaufer, announced she was having an affair with the former CEO. Welch and his second wife, Jane, divorced shortly after the affair came out in the news. Welch had married Jane in 1989 after divorcing his wife of thirty years, Carolyn, in 1987.

Despite this scandal, Welch's reputation as one of the most admired and well-known business leaders in U.S. history—and probably in the world—is likely to stay intact. *Newsweek* magacine, while questioning what the Wetlaufer affair would do to his reputation, noted that Welch was considered the best manager in the last 50 years—high praise for a business leader.

For More Information

Books

Campbell, Robert. *The Golden Years of Broadcasting: A Celebration of the First 50 Years of Radio and TV on NBC.* New York: Rutledge/Charles Scribner's Sons, 1976.

Slater, Robert. *The New GE: How Jack Welch Revised an American Institution.* Homewood, IL: Business One Irwin, 1993.

Sobel, Robert. *RCA.* Briarcliff Manor, NY: Stein and Day, 1986.

Weaver, Pat, with Thomas M. Coffey. *The Best Seat in the House: The Golden Years of Radio and Television.* New York: Alfred A. Knopf, 1994.

Welch, Jack, with John A. Byrne. *Jack: Straight from the Gut.* New York: Warner Books, 2001.

Periodicals

Gibney, Frank, Eric Roston, James Graff, and Joseph Kirwin. "How Jack Fell Down." *Time* (July 16, 2001): p. 40.

Jerome, Jim. "Electric General: The Corporate World's Boldest Boss, Jack Welch, Gears Up to Chill Out." *People Weekly* (November 5, 2001): p. 56.

Web Sites

General Electric, Inc. [On-line] http://www.ge.com (accessed on August 15, 2002).

National Broadcasting Corporation (NBC). [On-line] http://www.nbc.com (accessed on August 15, 2002).

General Motors Corporation

300 Renaissance Center
Detroit, MI 48265-3000
(313) 556-5000
http://www.gm.com

**General Motors
Corporation headquarters,
Detroit, Michigan.**
*Reproduced by permission of
AP/Wide World Photos.*

O ver the course of nearly a century, General Motors (GM) has weathered more ups and downs and gone through more fundamental changes than most companies. GM has been the world's largest vehicle manufacturer since 1931, producing such brands as Buick, Cadillac, Chevrolet, GMC, Pontiac, Saab, Saturn, and Oldsmobile. From the 1950s into the 1970s, the automaker led the industry in building millions of low-cost cars, achieving nearly 60 percent of U.S. auto sales. Along the way, its Chevy Corvette convertible sports car became an American icon and a symbol of the laid-back West Coast lifestyle. Today, General Motors has about 30 percent of the auto market and faces new challenges, such as decreased productivity, rising costs of employees health benefits, and the demand for cleaner, safer, and more fuel-efficient vehicles.

From Carriages to Cars

General Motors traces its history back to the late 1800s, when William "Billy" Durant (1861–1947) was leading the horse-drawn carriage market in Flint, Michigan. A natural born salesman with his finger on the pulse of new markets, he realized the future was in the "horseless" carriage. In 1904, Durant took over Flint's failing Buick Motor Company. He quickly turned Buick around, and by 1907, was producing over four thousand cars per year. In 1908, with Durant at the helm, the company was the number-one automaker in the United States, out-selling rivals Cadillac and **Ford Motor Company** (see entry).

Spurred by his success, Durant set out to take control of the auto industry. He attempted to buy Ford Motor Company in 1907, but was unable to obtain a $9.5 million bank loan. Instead, he formed the General Motors Company, with headquarters in Detroit, Michigan, and began adding other new divisions. In 1908, Durant purchased Olds Motor Works, which had been formed in 1899 by Ransom E. Olds (1864–1950). In 1909, he acquired the Oakland Motor Car Company, which eventually became the Pontiac division in 1932. Rapid Motor Vehicle Company, the predecessor of the GMC truck, was purchased soon after. By 1910, Durant had gobbled up so many companies that GM was deeply in debt and on the verge of financial collapse. Several banks stepped in with loans to help out the struggling automaker on the condition that founder Durant be replaced as company head. After losing control of GM, Durant started the Chevrolet Motor Company in 1911.

The General Motors board of directors elected Pierre S. du Pont (1870–1954) its chairman in 1915, a position he retained for nearly fourteen years. Durant, however, remained on the board and embarked on a GM stock-buying spree. By 1916, he had purchased 54.5 percent of GM stock and with a

General Motors at a Glance

- **Employees:** 362,000

- **CEO:** G. Richard Wagoner Jr.

- **Subsidiaries:** Adam Opel AG; Allison Transmission Division; Covisint, Inc.; Daewoo Motor Company Ltd.; General Motors Acceptance Corporation; GMAC Insurance; GM Locomotive Group; Hughes Electronic Company; Isuzu Motors Ltd.; New United Motor Manufacturing, Inc.; OnStar Corporation; Saab Automobile AB; Saturn Corporation; Vauxhall Motors Ltd.

- **Major Competitors:** DaimlerChrysler AG; Ford Motor Company; Toyota Motor Corporation; Honda

- **Notable Products:** Buick: Regal, Century, LeSabre; Cadillac: Seville, El Dorado, Escalade; Chevrolet: Blazer, Camaro, Corvette, Prizm, Silverado, Cavalier, Impala, Suburban, Tahoe; GMC: Sierra

 **Timeline**

1897: Olds Motor Vehicle Company is started by Ransom E. Olds.

1903: David B. Buick founds the Buick Motor Company.

1908: General Motors Corporation is formed, incorporating Buick and Olds.

1909: GM purchases Cadillac Automobile Company.

1918: GM buys the Chevrolet Motor Company.

1923: GM opens its first European assembly plant in Copenhagen, Denmark.

1932: Pontiac division is established.

1936: Workers at two Michigan assembly plants stage a sit-down strike.

1937: Workers' strike is settled when GM recognizes the United Auto Workers (UAW) union.

1942: All GM plants convert to producing military supplies until the end of World War II.

1953: GM introduces the Chevy Corvette.

1956: Chevrolet unveils the Corvair.

1965: Ralph Nader publishes the book, *Unsafe at Any Speed,* critical of GM and its Corvair.

1969: GM-made guidance and navigation systems are used in Apollo 11 Moon landing; Corvair is discontinued.

1985: GM acquires Hughes Aircraft Company.

1986: GM announces plans to close eleven U.S. plants.

1990: The Saturn line of cars is introduced.

1991: GM chairman Robert Stempel resigns amid financial crisis.

1999: Assembly plant is opened in Shanghai, China.

2000: GM announces it will discontinue its Oldsmobile line.

2002: Company announces that eighty-seven new models will be introduced over the next four years.

controlling interest, took over as president of GM, ousting Charles W. Nash (1864–1948) who had served in that role since 1912. Power shifted again in 1918, when General Motors took over Chevrolet.

Empire Thrives

General Motors expanded into Canada in 1918, merging the McLaughlin Motor Car Company Ltd. and Chevrolet Motor Company of Canada Ltd. into General Motors of Canada Ltd. It also made an attempt to get into aircraft manufacturing when it purchased the Dayton Wright Company in 1919. Ten years later, it sold the company to Fokker Aircraft Corporation. A more successful acquisition that year was of the Guardian Frigerator Company, which was renamed Frigidaire Corporation. It soon became the best-selling refrigerator in the country.

The 1920s and 1930s saw General Motors continue to expand by purchasing smaller companies and moving into foreign markets. It opened its first European assembly plant in Copenhagen, Denmark, in 1923. The first GM vehicle assembled outside the United States and Canada, a Chevrolet utility truck, rolled off the assembly line on January 7, 1924. Manufacturing plants were also opened in Buenos Aires, Argentina, in 1925, followed by plants in Australia and New Zealand in 1926. GM's acquisitions included Vauxhall Motors Ltd. of England, Fisher Body Company of Detroit, and Adam Opel AG of Germany.

In 1923, Alfred P. Sloan Jr. (1875–1966) became president of the ever-expanding GM. His priority was to make sure all the various divisions of the company were functioning efficiently. As part of this vision, Sloan structured General Motors so that its many parts worked together to produce maximum profits. At the same time, he wanted each of the divisions to retain its own unique identity. This was no easy task since GM produced a wide range of products, including Cadillac limousines, earthmoving equipment, buses, refrigerators, spark plugs, and roller bearings. For much of Sloan's long tenure, which lasted from 1923 until 1956, General Motors was the largest and most profitable manufacturing company in the world.

In 1936, amid the harsh economic climate of the Great Depression, employees at two GM plants in Flint staged sit-down strikes. Like many workers across the United States, they demanded higher wages, more benefits, and the right to be represented by a union. The strikes ended after about six weeks when GM recognized the United Auto Workers (UAW) union. Through the union, autoworkers could negotiate with their employees for improved working conditions, wages, work hours, and benefits.

On January 11, 1940, General Motors produced its twenty-five millionth vehicle but entered the decade under the dark cloud of World War II (1939–45). GM Japan ceased operation in 1941, the year the Japanese bombed Pearl Harbor. In 1942, GM converted all production at its assembly plants to the war effort, churning out $12.3 billion worth of goods, including airplanes, airplane engines and parts, trucks, tanks, guns, and ammunition shells. Vehicles included the 6x6 Army truck that carried troops and supplies and the DUKW, known as "the duck," which could carry fifty troops on land or water.

GM Tangles with Federal Government

With the war over, GM again turned to producing cars, bringing out several dozen new models in the 1950s and 1960s. An American legend was born in 1953 when GM introduced the Chevrolet Corvette, the first mass-produced sports car and the first with a plastic body. The company introduced new, smaller models during the 1960s, including the Buick Special, Oldsmobile F-85, Chevy II, and Pontiac Tempest.

The decade also found GM embroiled in several battles with the federal government. In 1961, the U.S. Department of Justice accused the company of using unfair practices to try and control all aspects of the diesel electric locomotive market. A federal judge dismissed the charge three years later. In 1962, the Justice Department filed charges against GM and three Chevrolet dealer trade associations. It accused GM of restricting Chevrolet sales in Southern California by refusing to sell to " discount houses," which are independent car dealers that buy vehicles in bulk and resell them to the public, usually at lower prices. A federal court ruled against GM in 1966, ordering it to stop restricting sales of Chevrolets to discount houses.

The company's image was further tarnished in 1965 with the release of *Unsafe at Any Speed,* a landmark book written by consumer advocate Ralph Nader (1934–). In his book, Nader was highly critical of GM and its Corvair model, which resulted in a publicized ongoing disagreement between the advocate and the automaker. In 1966, Nader accused GM of harassment, and the U.S. Senate committee investigated the sit-

Beetle Invasion Spurs Ill-fated Corvair

In the mid-1950s, the Volkswagen Beetle was a big hit in the United States and GM's Chevrolet division decided it needed a car to compete with it. Chevy designers were told to come up with a car that was small, got good gas mileage, was easy to manufacture, and had a European look. The result was the Corvair, which debuted in 1960, and was available as either a two-door coupe or a four-door sedan. In appearance, it was not at all like the Beetle. It had a boxy shape compared to the VW's half dome look. It also had more interior room. It did, however, incorporate many of the basic components of the Beetle, including an engine located in the rear of the vehicle.

By 1965, more than 1.2 million Corvairs had been sold when the car ran head-on into a wall of bad publicity. That year, the book *Unsafe at Any Speed* by consumer advocate Ralph Nader (1934–), was published. It claimed the Corvair would sometimes malfunction, causing the car to go out of control and roll over. GM denied there was a safety problem and in 1972, the National Highway Safety Administration investigated the situation and found that the Corvair was safe. The ruling, however, came too late. In 1965, Chevrolet produced 237,000 Corvairs; that number dropped to 103,000 in 1966. In 1969, the last year the car was built, only 6,000 Corvairs came down the assembly line. Over one million snazzy Corvairs were produced between 1960 and 1969; an estimated 300,000 Corvairs were still in use in 2002.

uation. Company president James M. Roche acknowledged the harassment and apologized to Nader on behalf of GM. In 1969, GM's Chevrolet division announced it was discontinuing Corvair production.

The 1970s brought a whole new set of problems. With the start of the environmental movement, public pressure was placed on the U.S. government to reduce air pollution. As a result, federal laws were created that required Detroit to build "cleaner" cars. In 1971, GM introduced engines that ran on unleaded or low-leaded gasoline, which burned cleaner than fully leaded gasoline. Prior to that time, all cars ran on leaded gas. In order to comply with the Federal Clean Air Act, GM began installing catalytic converters on all its cars sold in the United States and Canada, beginning with 1975 models. Catalytic converters help clean harmful exhaust fumes emitted by cars. It also began to build smaller cars that used fuel more efficiently, a trend that continued through the 1980s. That trend was reversed in the 1990s with the rise in popularity of bigger vehicles, particularly minivans and sport utility vehicles (SUVs).

Company Heads for Financial Collapse

By the start of 1980, the United States economy was in trouble. As a result, auto sales plummeted and carmakers suffered. GM posted an annual financial loss that year, its first since 1920. The loss came at a time when the company was spending billions of dollars to modernize aging assembly plants in the United States and abroad. Its finances were also weakened by a string of acquisitions made during the decade, including Hughes Aircraft Company, a defense electronics firm, and Electronic Data Systems, a data processing and telecommunications company. These factors led GM to close eleven plants worldwide, including several much publicized closings in Flint, Michigan, the city where the company began. All told, thirty thousand jobs were eliminated. The cost-cutting moves seemed to have paid off when in 1988, GM reported a $4.9 billion profit on record sales of $110.2 billion.

The sweeping and painful cuts were put in place by GM head Roger B. Smith (1925–), the longest-running CEO since Sloan. Smith was a colorful but controversial person who added an interesting chapter to the history of GM. Named CEO in 1981, he became known for his extraordinary vision and business savvy. He was also considered to be a blunt, quick-tempered loner. Smith expanded GM's overseas operations and improved the quality of GM cars. He served as CEO until he retired in 1990.

The 1990s, like the 1980s, was a decade of turmoil for General Motors. As revenues once again dropped, GM chairman Robert Stempel (1933–) announced he would close twenty-one North American production plants and eliminate seventy-four thousand jobs over four years as a cost-cutting measure. But the cuts failed to impress GM's board of directors, which demanded and received Stempel's resignation, giving the job of CEO, and the daunting task of rebuilding the company, to John F. "Jack" Smith Jr. The bright spot of the decade for GM was the introduction of the Saturn line of autos, built in Tennessee. The Saturn was designed to compete against small import cars, which it did with great success. Part of the success was due to Saturn dealerships not employing high-pressure sales techniques and its excellent customer service.

On the Upswing

After twenty years of declining market share, General Motors started the twenty-first century with a shakeup of its top management. Its board of directors named G. Richard Wagoner Jr. as its CEO in 2000, replacing Smith, who remained as chairman of the board. Some industry analysts suggested GM would have been better off hiring a more dynamic leader from outside the company. According to Irene Gashurov writing for *Fortune* magazine in 2000, "Despite constant reorganization over the past decade, [GM] remains complex, bureaucratic, and highly politicized. The question is not so much, Can Rick Wagoner run GM? He can. The questions are these: Can Rick Wagoner make GM hum? Can he turn it once more into the heartbeat of America? Can any insider?"

Two years later, those questions were at least initially answered. By 2001, after several decades of decline, GM controlled 30.9 percent of the U.S. auto market, up slightly over 2000. That same year, the company reported a profit of $1.5 billion on global sales of $177.3 billion. Some of the biggest news came in 2002 when, for the first time in eleven years, Chevrolet vehicles outsold Ford. Some industry analysts credited the upswing to improved vehicle quality, increased worker productivity, and getting rid of unprofitable vehicles. GM also unveiled plans for introducing more models than ever before, with eighty-seven new car models to roll out between 2002 and 2006. The success of GM will likely hinge on how popular these new models become.

Roger & Me

The closing of GM plants in Flint, Michigan, led to the 1989 controversial movie *Roger & Me* by Michael Moore (1964–), a novice filmmaker and son of a Flint GM worker. The film features Moore relentlessly pursuing Roger B. Smith (1925–), CEO and chairman of General Motors, to try and get him to visit Flint, which was devastated by the shutdown of the GM factories. Funny in parts and deeply moving in others, the movie tells the story of a working-class city in the Midwest that depended on the auto industry.

Jack Smith.
Reproduced by permission of Corbis Corporation (Bellevue).

Jack Smith

Born: April 6, 1938
Stamford, Connecticut
Chairman of the board, General Motors Corporation

"At General Motors, we have made many unprecedented and controversial changes since 1992, when we stared financial Armageddon in the eye. However, despite the financial turnaround and all the other progress, we are still not where we need to be on the journey."

For Jack Smith, the journey has taken place on a long and winding road filled with bumps and potholes. So far, he has been able to guide General Motors (GM) around the obstacles, taking it from near financial ruin in 1992 to a more efficiently run operation in 2002. Before the widely publicized management and board shakeup at GM in 1992, few people outside the automobile industry had heard of Smith. Since then, his face has graced the front pages of newspapers and magazine covers nationwide. In January of 1994, he was even seated beside First Lady Hillary Rodham Clinton (1947–) as President Bill Clinton (1946–) delivered the annual State of the Union address.

Family Politics

John F. Smith Jr., known as Jack, was born on April 6, 1938, the second of John and Eleanor Sullivan Smith's four children. The Smiths had high expectations for their children, and disciplined them firmly. Perhaps they had to since Jack, sisters Mary and Sally, and younger brother Michael waged a near constant battle of sibling rivalry. The family lived in a middle-class neighborhood in Worcester, Massachusetts, where Eleanor Sullivan's large Irish family was active in city politics. The Sullivans were well represented on the city's police force, and Eleanor's brother, Charles "Jeff" Sullivan, was mayor of Worcester in the late 1940s. He later served as the lieutenant governor of Massachusetts. Jack Smith often accompanied his uncle on whistle-stop train tours, passing out handbills and attending campaign-related events.

Smith learned the concept of teamwork from his father, John, and paternal uncles. John Smith, a quiet, patient man, was director of the city's public health department, and co-owner with his two brothers of Smithfield Famous Ice Cream, a chain of eight parlors in the area. Jack Jr. learned the principles of business at the ice cream parlors, pitching in to make ice cream and helping to run the various stores. As an adult, Smith kept a replica of one of Smithfield's delivery trucks in his office.

Jack Smith attended Blessed Sacrament Grammar School through the eighth grade, then went to St. John Prep School, an elite private high school dedicated exclusively to education. Between his studies and working after school, he had little time for sports and extracurricular activities. After graduating from high school, Smith attended the University of Massachusetts, where he received his bachelor's degree in business administration in 1960. He then went on to Boston University to pursue an advanced business degree.

Climbs the Ranks at GM

Smith spent most of his GM career outside Detroit, Michigan. He joined GM in 1961 as a payroll auditor at the Fisher Body plant in Framingham, Massachusetts. Around that time he married Marie Holloway, his high-school sweetheart, and commuted to Boston University to complete his master's of business administration (MBA), which he received in 1965. Five years later Smith moved to the GM treasurer's office, and by 1974 he had worked his way up to assistant treasurer. Smith was transferred to Detroit in 1976, when he was promoted to assistant comptroller; four years later, he became comptroller.

Wagoner: Always in the Game

G. Richard Wagoner Jr., or Rick Wagoner, as his associates know him, is definitely more than a coach on the sidelines. As chief executive officer (CEO) of General Motors (GM), the third largest company in the world in 2002, he is always in the game, whether he is acting as a coach, player, manager, or cheerleader. He took the helm of GM as it moved out of the 1990s, a decade of turbulence, when the company was in danger of financial collapse.

Wagoner was born on February 9, 1953, in Wilmington, Delaware, but grew up in Richmond, Virginia. He entered North Carolina's Duke University in 1971, where he played forward on the basketball team from 1971 to 1972. Although Wagoner did not believe he had what it took to play college or professional basketball, he became a lifelong fan of the game, especially rooting for the Duke Blue Devils. After graduating with his bachelor's degree in economics in 1975, Wagoner immediately entered Harvard University's business program, graduating in 1977.

After Wagoner earned his master's of business administration (MBA), he was hired

G. Richard Wagoner Jr.
Reproduced by permission of AP/Wide World Photos.

by the New York treasurer's office of General Motors, where he worked as an analyst and was soon noticed for doing an exceptional job. Beginning in 1981, he spent some time in Brazil as treasurer of GM do Brasil. After a brief return to the United States, Wagoner spent a year as a vice president and finance manager at GM Canada in 1987. Remaining in Canada, he spent two years as director of

In 1982, Smith was named director of worldwide product planning, his first GM job that allowed him to showcase his abilities beyond number crunching. Smith took on the ambitious task of negotiating a joint venture between General Motors and Japan's Toyota Motor Corporation. In 1984, the deal was strategic business planning for Chevrolet-Pontiac-GM of the Canada group. During this time, Wagoner learned every aspect of the automotive business, although he remained primarily a financial expert.

Wagoner was promoted to vice president in charge of finance of GM Europe in 1989 and was also named to GM's board of directors. Although financial concerns remained at the core of his duties, he also showed ability to soothe tensions between various factions in the company. Wagoner smoothed over ruffled feathers among British, German, and Swiss units, and got them to work together, instead of being at odds. In 1991, Wagoner returned to South America when he was named president of GM do Brasil. There, he focused on global purchasing, implemented cost-cutting programs, and encouraged production to focus on more modern models of GM cars. Wagoner accomplished so much that he was one of only two top executives to get bonuses that year.

In the early 1990s, Wagoner came back to the United States. Although he was only thirty-nine years old, he was named chief financial officer (CFO) of GM in 1992. In 1994, Wagoner was promoted again, to president of GM's North American operations. This made him second in command at GM. The company faced numerous problems: the division was losing money, market share was down, and GM made less per car than every other major automotive manufacturer. Wagoner went on a cost-cutting spree. He also reinvented how GM conducted business. Under his command, North American operations broke even.

In 1998, Wagoner was named president and chief operating officer (COO) of the newly created GM Automotive Operations. This combined the North American operations with GM operations around the world. Wagoner worked to streamline the company and enact more cost savings so it could respond better to world markets. He also insisted that manufacturing techniques be changed and updated. Wagoner had a plan to slowly update every aspect of GM. He earned his highest promotion in 2000 when he was named president and CEO of GM, the youngest person to hold this position since the company was founded.

closed and New United Motors Manufacturing Inc. was formed. The factory was co-owned and operated by GM and Toyota, and was based in Fremont, California. During negotiations, Smith visited several Toyota plants in Japan. He became convinced that Toyota's production methods were GM's ticket to the future.

Smith was promoted to president of GM of Canada in 1984, and in 1986 became chief of GM's passenger car division in Europe. The overseas move helped contribute to Jack and Marie Holloway Smith's divorce. The marriage's fate was sealed when Smith accepted the job as GM's second-ranking executive in Europe, one of the most difficult assignments at GM at the time. The couple divorced in 1986.

Smith benefited both professionally and personally during his years in Europe. While there, he met Lydia Sigrist, a Swiss secretary for GM who was also divorced and raising a teenage daughter. The attraction was instant, but the two agreed they could not date as long as both of them worked for the same company. Sigrist left GM and took on the task of transforming the auto executive. She encouraged Smith to lose forty pounds, took him hiking in the mountains, and helped him trade in his rumpled dressing habits for more stylish suits and ties. The couple married in August 1988, a few weeks after Smith was transferred back to Detroit as executive vice president for international operations.

Reaches Top of Corporate Ladder

Two years later, Smith was named vice chairman of GM with responsibility for international operations. Meanwhile, some members of the GM board of directors, led by John Smale, an attorney and retired **Procter & Gamble Company** (see entry) CEO, were growing increasingly unhappy with GM's management team under CEO Robert Stempel (1933–) and president Lloyd Reuss. Becoming more impatient with GM's mounting losses in the United States, Canada, and Mexico, they began demanding answers to questions, such as why the cost-cutting measures that helped turn around GM Europe could not be applied to North America.

In April of 1992, the directors demoted Reuss and other top GM executives, and named Smith president and chief operating officer (COO). His appointed task was to save GM's ailing North American operations, which lost an estimated $11.4 billion in the previous two years. He became president and CEO of GM on November 2, 1992, after former chairman and CEO Robert Stempel resigned.

Smith's promotion surprised some, even though he had a strong track record. He was known inside GM as the low-key, but capable executive who turned the company's struggling European operations into the company's crown jewel. In 2000, Smith was replaced as CEO, but remained chairman of the board of directors. He was heralded as the man who might be able to turn the manufacturing giant into a leaner and more profitable company. His goal in the twenty-first century was to regain some of the market share GM lost to Ford, **DaimlerChrysler AG** (see entry), Toyota, and even Honda, in the 1980s and 1990s.

For More Information

Books

Madsen, Alan. *The Deal Maker: How William C. Durant Made General Motors.* New York: John Wiley & Sons, 1999.

Maynard, Micheline. *Collision Course: Inside the Battle for General Motors.* New York: Birch Lane Press, 1995.

Nader, Ralph. *Unsafe at Any Speed.* 1965. Reprint, New York: Knightsbridge Publishing Company, 1991.

Sloan, Alfred P. *My Years with General Motors.* New York: Doubleday, 1996.

Periodicals

Brooke, Lindsay. "The New Playmaker." *Automotive Industries* (February 2001): p. 26.

"The Future Direction of General Motors." *Automotive Manufacturing & Production* (September 1998): pp. 28–34.

Gashurov, Irene. "GM's Big Decision: Status Quo: Can an Insider Jump-start the World's Largest Corporation?" *Fortune* (February 21, 2000): p. 100.

"GM's Motor Man." *The Economist* (March 18, 2000): p. 69.

Meredith, Robyn. "Digital Drive." *Forbes* (May 29, 2000): p. 128.

Taylor, Alex, III. "Finally GM is Looking Good." *Fortune* (April 1, 2002): p. 68.

———. "GM Keeps Its Game Face On." *Fortune* (October 15, 2001): p. 98.

———. "Is Jack Smith the Man to Fix GM?" *Fortune* (August 3, 1998): pp. 86–91.

Witzenburg, Gary. "A Diamond for the General: Big Business Gets Better as GM Reaches its 75th Anniversary." *Motor Trend* (December 1983): pp. 128–134.

Web Sites

Buick. [On-line] http://www.buick.com (accessed on August 15, 2002).

Chevrolet. [On-line] http://www.chevrolet.com (accessed on August 15, 2002).

General Motors Corporation. [On-line] http://www.gm.com (accessed on August 15, 2002).

Oldsmobile. [On-line] http://www.oldsmobile.com (accessed on August 15, 2002).

Pontiac. [On-line] http://www.pontiac.com (accessed on August 15, 2002).

Hallmark Cards, Inc.

2501 McGee Street
Kansas City, MO 64108
(816) 274-5111
www.hallmark.com

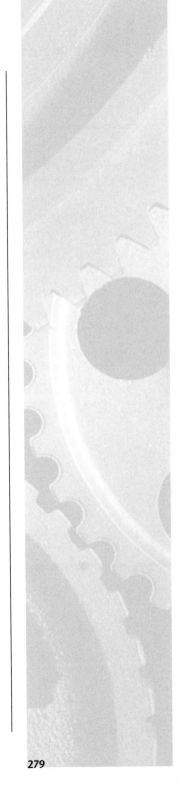

When three brothers decided to get into the greeting card business more than ninety years ago, very few people exchanged cards. Today, greeting cards have become big business with Hallmark Cards, Inc. leading the pack. Hallmark produces almost four billion cards a year, nearly half of all cards sold in the United States. Contributing to sales is the fact that the company "invented" dozens of holidays, from Secretary's Day and Bosses Day to Grandmother's Day and Mother-in-Law Day, with a line of cards especially designed for each event. There are even cards for your pet's birthday and electronic cards that play music.

From Postcards to Greeting Cards

Hallmark first began in 1910 when founder Joyce C. Hall started selling postcards from his room at the YMCA in Kansas City, Missouri. He moved the business into a rented office later that year after the YMCA complained about the large volume of mail he was generating. In 1911, he and his two brothers, William and Rollie, formed Hall Brothers. The brothers

Hallmark at a Glance

- **Employees:** 20,000

- **CEO:** Donald J. Hall Jr.

- **Subsidiaries:** Binney & Smith, Inc.; Crown Center Redevelopment Corporation; Crown Media Holdings, Inc.; DaySpring Cards, Inc.; Gift Certificate Center; Hallmark Entertainment, Inc.; Halls Merchandising, Inc.; Image Arts; InterArt; Irrestible Ink, Inc.; Litho-Krome Company; The Picture People; Tapper Candies, Inc.; William Arthur

- **Major Competitors:** American Greetings; CSS Industries; Viacom; Blue Mountain Arts

- **Notable Products:** Hallmark cards; Ambassador cards; Fresh Ink cards; Crayola crayons; Silly Putty; Portfolio Series arts materials; *Hallmark Hall of Fame* television programs; the Hallmark Channel

started selling greeting cards in 1912 as the popularity of postcards began to decline. Two years later, the company began designing its own cards, creating twenty engraved Christmas card designs. But disaster struck in 1915 when a fire destroyed their office and their entire inventory, including unfulfilled Valentine card orders, leaving the company $17,000 in debt.

The brothers quickly rebounded, setting up shop in a new office with their own engraving presses on which they printed their own cards. In 1916, they opened their first retail store in Kansas City. The following year, Hall Brothers designed a humorous greeting card and began producing and selling the first Christmas gift-wrapping paper. In 1919, the company moved to a larger building in Kansas City to accommodate its growing workforce, which numbered twenty-five. They also introduced a line of friendship cards.

During the national prosperity of the 1920s, Hall Brothers rapidly expanded, adding several hundred employees, including more than a dozen full-time artists. The trademark name "Hallmark" first appeared on the back of cards in 1925. The product line expanded to include Christmas and other decorative seals, party invitations, birth announcements, calendars, and sympathy cards. Hallmark advertisements also appeared for the first time, in the *Ladies Home Journal*.

The Hallmark Way

The 1930s saw the company continue to grow, despite the worldwide economic depression. Hall Brothers began offer-

Timeline

1910: Joyce C. Hall starts a wholesale postcard business in Kansas City, Missouri.

1911: Hall Brothers is formed.

1915: Hall Brothers begins printing their own greeting cards.

1919: Friendship cards are introduced by the company.

1925: The word "Hallmark" first appears on cards.

1932: Hallmark licenses the rights to use Walt Disney characters.

1951: The first *Hallmark Hall of Fame* television program airs.

1954: Hall Brothers officially changes its name to Hallmark Cards, Inc.

1966: Donald J. Hall becomes president and CEO.

1977: Irvine O. Hockaday joins the company's board of directors.

1982: Joyce C. Hall dies at the age of ninety-one.

1984: Hallmark acquires Binney & Smith, makers of Crayola crayons.

1996: Hallmark Entertainment Network is formed.

2002: Donald J. Hall Jr. becomes CEO, replacing Hockaday, who retires.

ing its employees benefits almost unheard of at the time, including retirement pensions, health care, life insurance, regular coffee breaks, and paid vacations. It was the start of Hallmark's philosophy that employees are the company's most valuable resource.

As a matter of fact, many corporate analysts attribute much of Hallmark's continued success to the way it treats its employees. Over the years, workers were offered a profit-sharing program and a stock ownership plan. The company is privately held, with employees owning about a quarter of the stock. Other current worker benefits include six months of unpaid parental leave, financial help in adopting children, and sick childcare leave. Hallmark often has made the top spot on several lists, including one compiled by *Working Mother* magazine that ranks the most admired and most employee-friendly companies in the United States.

Offering the Very Best

During the 1930s, W. E. Coutts Company became Hall Brothers' Canadian affiliate, or partner. The company also entered into a licensing deal with the **Walt Disney Company** (see entry) to feature such Disney characters as Mickey Mouse and Donald Duck on its cards. This was a first for both companies. In 1936, Hall Brothers again moved to a larger building in Kansas City to house its nearly eight hundred workers. It also introduced new products during the decade such as cellophane wrapping and silk-screen cards.

The company continued to thrive during the 1940s despite World War II (1939–45), opening manufacturing plants in Topeka and Leavenworth, Kansas. In 1944, Hall Brothers introduced its now famous slogan, "When you care enough to send the very best." It also began sponsoring the wartime radio show, "Meet Your Navy."

As American culture transferred from radio to television, Hallmark also made the jump. Hall, however, was not satisfied with the quality of television programming and decided that instead of just buying advertising spots, Hallmark would produce and sponsor its own shows. In 1951, Hallmark debuted *Amahl and the Night Visitors*, the first original opera created specifically for television. It marked the beginning of a series of television specials that later became the *Hallmark Hall of Fame*.

After nearly forty years of being known as Hall Brothers or Hallmark, the company officially changed its name to Hallmark Cards, Inc. in 1954. By the time the company turned fifty years old in 1960, Joyce Hall's son, Donald J. Hall, entered the ranks of company management as assistant to the president. In addition, the continued growth of Hallmark forced the company to move to larger headquarters in Kansas City to accommodate its workforce of more than four thousand, including 350 artists. Hallmark was producing four million cards a day, and introducing fifteen thousand new products and designs each year.

Critical Acclaim for *Hallmark Hall of Fame*

Upset with the quality of early television, Hallmark founder Joyce C. Hall decided to do something. In the early 1950s, he set about creating a series of programs based on some of history's most critically acclaimed books, stage plays, and operas. The first was the world premier presentation of the opera *Amahl and the Night Visitors* by Gian Carlo Menotti (1911–), which aired on Christmas Eve 1951. In 1953, Hallmark debuted William Shakespeare's *Hamlet*. It was the first time a Shakespeare play was aired on TV.

Although the series maintained a focus on the classics, it also expanded to include socially relevant stories written specifically for television. These intimate portraits included *Teacher, Teacher* (1969), the story of a mentally challenged youth, and *My Name is Bill W.* (1989), which tells the story of the founding of Alcoholics Anonymous. The program continues into the twenty-first century with such offerings as *The Runaway* (2000), about two boys dealing with racial prejudice in post-World War II Georgia, and *Follow the Stars Home* (2001), the story of a single mother raising a disabled child.

Over the years, the *Hall of Fame* original programs have won eighty-seven Emmy Awards, the highest honor given in television. Among the award-winning programs are *Jason and the Argonauts* (2000) and the great sea epic *Moby-Dick* (1998), written by Herman Melville (1819–1891). The roster of stars that have appeared in Hallmark productions include Katharine Hepburn (1907–), Paul Newman (1925–), Sidney Poitier (1927–), and Tommy Lee Jones (1946–).

Cleaning House

The 1960s brought about changes in the corporate leadership of Hallmark, although the company remained a family affair. Donald J. Hall was named president and chief executive officer (CEO), replacing his father, Joyce, who remained chairman of the board of directors. Continued growth spurred the company to build a new manufacturing plant in Topeka, Kansas, and expand its Lawrence, Kansas, facility to 450,000 square feet. The company was also doing well globally, which led it to form a subsidiary, Hallmark International.

In the mid-1960s, Joyce Hall became concerned about the deteriorating conditions in the Kansas City neighborhood where Hallmark's corporate headquarters were located. When city officials failed to take notice Hall decided to act on his own.

In 1966, he retired as CEO in order to devote more time to the issue. Two years later he began construction of the Crown Center, a residential, retail, and commercial real estate development designed to halt urban decay in the neighborhood.

Part of the complex, which included office space, opened in 1971. The first phase was fully completed in 1973 and included a shopping mall, Westin Crown Center Hotel, and the Crown Center Ice Terrace. The first phase of Crown Center's residential community was completed in 1976 with the opening of the San Francisco Tower Condominiums and Santa Fe Place Apartments.

New Blood

In 1986, after Donald Hall had been running the company for twenty years, Hallmark's board of directors thought it was time to select a CEO from outside the family. It turned to Irvine O. Hockaday Jr., who had joined the company in 1977. When Hockaday was appointed CEO, it marked the first time that Hallmark did not have a Hall family member at the helm. Some industry observers believed that bringing in an outsider might cause friction among the company's old guard.

It seemed, however, that new blood was exactly what Hallmark needed. Hockaday was quickly accepted by the other top executives and led the company through one of its most dynamic periods. Under Hockaday, Hallmark went on a corporate buying binge, purchasing Litho-Krome, a printing company based in Columbus, Georgia, and The Specialty Press Ltd., an Australian greeting card manufacturer. It also bought Dawson Printing Company in New Zealand. The Litho-Krome acquisition gave the company a quality printing plant in the South. The other two purchases bolstered Hallmark's international presence, allowing the company to cut costs by producing cards directly in Australia and New Zealand.

The 1980s saw Hallmark continue to grow, helped by the purchase of Binney & Smith, Inc., makers of Crayola crayons, in 1984. The company also expanded its product line, introducing Shoebox Greetings, an offbeat line of cards aimed at young, hip adults, and Mahogany, greeting cards designed for African Americans.

Hallmark continued its buying spree into the 1990s when it acquired several more companies, including Mundi-Paper, a Spanish greeting card manufacturer, and RHI Entertainment, a television programming and distribution firm. In 1996, RHI was renamed the Hallmark Entertainment Network, and given the mission to produce and distribute miniseries and movies made for television, including programs for the *Hallmark Hall of Fame.* It also operated the Hallmark Channel, a twenty-four-hour cable network dedicated to family programming. Other acquisitions during the 1990s included William Arthur, a producer of stationery products; Irresistible Ink, Inc., a direct-mail company; Tapper Candies of Cleveland, Ohio; and DaySpring Cards, Inc., an Arkansas-based maker of Christian-themed greeting cards.

Back in the Family

Hallmark made a change in leadership in 2002 when Donald J. Hall Jr. was named president and CEO, replacing Hockaday, who retired. The move came after the company experienced a drop in revenues from $4.3 billion in 2000 to $4 billion in 2001. For the first time in sixteen years, a member of the Hall family was again at the reins, and industry observers watched to see if Hall Jr. could do the job. "Skill set is really the measure here," said Paul Karofsky of Northeastern University's School of Business in a 2001 *Chief Executive* article. "And there's an obligation of family to perform to a higher standard."

The biggest competition Hallmark and other greeting card companies faced in the early twenty-first century was the Internet, where consumers could log on to such sites as

Hallmark Wrangles with Blue Mountain

Hallmark ran into legal problems in 1986 when greeting card creator Susan Polis Schutz and her husband Stephen sued the company for copyright infringement. The couple, owners of Blue Mountain Arts of Boulder, Colorado, claimed Hallmark had been using their designs on its cards without permission or payment. The U.S. Supreme Court refused to hear the case in 1988, allowing a lower court ruling against Hallmark to stand. The company agreed to buy back hundreds of thousands of Schutz-inspired cards from Hallmark retail shops and pay the couple an undisclosed amount. Writer Susan and artist Stephen founded Blue Mountain Arts in 1970 as a small specialty greeting card manufacturer. Today, although it still creates paper cards, Blue Mountain has become a household name thanks mostly to the popularity of its Web site www.bluemountain.com, where browsers can send free e-cards to friends and family.

The display Joyce C. Hall introduced when he first started selling cards is still used in Hallmark stores today.
Reproduced by permission of AP/Wide World Photos.

www.bluemountain.com and send electronic greeting cards, often accompanied by music, for free. Another challenge was getting to know and understand the new card-buying public. According to a 1999 article in *Time* magazine, "Female [baby] boomers buy cards, but they're quite diverse in sensibility and ethnicity, so the one-size-fits-all approach isn't working." The article further commented that, "For Generations X and Y, paper cards may as well be stone tablets."

To counteract this shift, Hallmark introduced a line of ninety-nine-cent cards to attract customers who were put off by growing paper card price tags. The company also added electronic card and gift options to its Internet site. In addition, Hallmark tended to rely less on its ten thousand retail shops (most run as independent franchises) and more on large discount chains, such as **Kmart** and **Wal-Mart** (see entries), and supermarkets and drugstore chains. But regardless of whether the cards are paper or electronic, or are sold in a small specialty shop or a mass-market chain, Hallmark is likely to remain the leader in the greeting card industry. It will do so because of its philosophy toward its employees and customers, which can be summed up in the verse that appeared on the very first Hallmark card in 1916: "I'd like to be the kind of friend you are to me."

Joyce C. Hall.
Reproduced by permission of Archive Photos, Inc.

Joyce C. Hall

Born: August 29, 1891
David City, Nebraska
Died: Oct. 29, 1982
Kansas City, Missouri
Founder and CEO, Hallmark Cards, Inc.

"If a man goes into business with only the idea of making a lot of money, chances are he won't. But if he puts service and quality first, the money will take care of itself. Producing a first-class product that is a real need is a much stronger motivation for success than getting rich."

Joyce C. Hall always put quality first, whether it came to products, customers, or employees. Because of this, Hall, a high school dropout, was able to build a multibillion-dollar greeting card empire that diversified into a wide variety of products and services, including residential and commercial property, art supplies, gift wrap and accessories, and television programming. In less than one hundred years, Hallmark went from a tiny post-card shop in Kansas City, Missouri, to the world's largest manufacturer and distributor of greeting cards, with thousands of retail outlets around the globe and annual sales of $4 billion.

A Boy Named Joyce

Joyce Clyde Hall was born on August 29, 1891, in the tiny farm town of David City, Nebraska. He was the youngest of three sons born to George Nelson Hall, a preacher, and Nancy Dudley Houston Hall. George and Nancy Hall were very religious, using the name of a Methodist bishop, Isaac W. Joyce, when it came time to christen their youngest boy. When Joyce Hall was just a child, his father died. Hall and his siblings, older brothers Rollie and William and younger sister Marie, were raised by their semi-invalid mother.

Hall went to work at the age of eight. A year later, his entrepreneurial talent already showed. He was only nine when he began to sell cosmetics and soap door-to-door for the California Perfume Company, which later became **Avon Products, Inc.** (see entry). When Hall was ten years old, the family moved to Norfolk, Nebraska, where Rollie and William had purchased a book and stationery store. In 1905, a Chicago salesman visited the store and convinced Hall that there was money to be made in selling postcards. Hall, then sixteen, invested his life savings of about $170 into the venture and convinced Rollie and William each to match his investment.

After a fire destroyed the Hall brothers' shop in 1915, they quickly moved to new headquarters and started over. One of the first original designs they created after the fire was a card featuring a drawing of a rope with a knot at the end. The inscription read, "When you get to the end of your rope, tie a knot and hang on." The modern version of that card shows a cat dangling from a rope with the message shortened to, "Hang in there, baby."

Together, they founded the Norfolk Post Card Company, importing foreign postcards and selling them to local merchants. During the school year, Hall was the company's order filler and card sorter. During vacations he took to the streets, selling both the postcards and a sawdust sweeping compound. The business struggled to survive and in 1910, Hall dropped out of high school and moved to Kansas City, Missouri, with a suitcase of clothes and two shoeboxes of postcards. He began selling the cards to drugstores, bookstores, and gift shops. Hall's brother Rollie joined him in 1911 and they opened a small book, card, and gift shop in downtown Kansas City, buying products designed and manufactured elsewhere and selling them wholesale.

Company and Business Leader

Although the business was a brotherly effort, Joyce Hall was the company's backbone. He constantly looked for ways to modernize things and kept his finger on the pulse of public tastes. Through the 1920s, Hall expanded the inventory to include

Joyce C. Hall used his greeting cards and his successful business to further the fine arts. The Hallmark Gallery Artists Christmas cards featured works by such great masters as Michelangelo (1475–1564), Leonardo da Vinci (1452–1519), and Rembrandt (1606–1669). Hall hoped these cards would bring the art of celebrated painters to people who would not ordinarily see them. He also created the International Hallmark Art Awards, providing funds to artists worldwide, and acquired famous works for the Hallmark Fine Arts Collection.

Christmas and other decorative seals, party invitations, sympathy cards, and calendars, all of which were big hits with customers in a time of economic boom. But Hall also paid attention to his personal life. On March 25, 1922, he married family friend Elizabeth Ann Didlay. They had three children, Elizabeth Ann, Barbara Louise, and Donald Joyce.

In the 1930s, Hall introduced a number of new marketing and sales strategies, such as an automatic reorder system, and self-service open display racks. Previously, cards were kept behind the sales counter and customers had to have a clerk pick out choices for them. People loved being able to sort through the cards on their own, and business soared.

The decade also brought the Great Depression, which devastated the nation's economy. Hall worked hard to ensure that his employees would keep their jobs. He was also dedicated to returning prosperity to the United States. The 1930 Joyce Hall Prosperity Plan was embraced and promoted by Rotary Clubs throughout the country. Rotary Clubs are community-based business organizations. The plan encouraged suppliers and customers to buy materials in advance, providing working capital for companies. According to Hall, his plan allowed people to keep working and earning wages. It also kept the spending cycle going. Some newspapers credited Hall and his plan with aiding the country's eventual economic recovery.

During the 1950s, Hall took a stand against the Cold War-era threat of nuclear destruction, and became involved in a peacekeeping effort. In 1956, President Dwight D. Eisenhower (1890–1969) invited Hall and other prominent American businessmen to the White House for an important discussion. The meeting concerned establishing an organization to promote world peace. The resulting organization was called People-to-People. It was an effort to foster mutual understanding, respect, and friendship between American citizens and citizens of the world. Hall served on the group's board of directors and was chairman

Hockaday Rings in New Century at Hallmark

During his sixteen years as Hallmark's chief executive officer (CEO), Irvine O. Hockaday helped move the company into the twenty-first century. He also helped position the company as a leader in entertainment, overseeing the launch of the Hallmark Entertainment Network, which has become one of the world's top creators of movies and miniseries for television. During his time with the company, revenues nearly tripled and the Hallmark brand prospered.

Hockaday was born August 12, 1936, in Ludington, Michigan. He graduated from Princeton University with a bachelor of arts degree in 1958, and in 1961, he earned a law degree from the University of Michigan. He joined Kansas City Southern Industries, Inc., in 1968 and served as its president and CEO from 1971 to 1983. Hockaday's involvement with Hallmark dates back to 1977 when he was elected to Hallmark's board of directors. In 1986, he became the first person outside the Hall family to be named president and CEO. When Hockaday retired from Hallmark in 2002, he was praised by his successor, Donald J. Hall Jr., grandson of founder Joyce C. Hall: "We are extremely grateful for his leadership during a dynamic period in our company's history."

of People-to-People's executive committee. During his service, he made several trips overseas to promote the peace initiative.

A few years later, Hall started the Hallmark Corporate Foundation, a nonprofit group that provides funds to Kansas City-area organizations and schools. The foundation's gifts have included grants to the University of Kansas to establish a business professorship and a design professorship, and annual scholarships for students at the Kansas City Art Institute.

Never Slowing Down

Hall's outside activities took up much of his time and he found that he was less able to focus his attention on running a company. He gradually weaned himself away from managing day-to-day operations of Hallmark, finally retiring as CEO in 1966. Hall continued to serve as chairman of the company's board of directors, but he soon found a new interest: land development. The urban decay surrounding Hallmark's Kansas

City headquarters bothered him and when the city failed to take action, Hall launched the redevelopment himself. Within ten years, he had built the 85-acre Crown Center. The residential, office, hotel, and entertainment district brought renewed interest to the area, and revitalization spread to nearby neighborhoods.

Because of his work with Crown Center and his charitable activities, Hall never totally retired. Not one to drop out of sight, he also continued to keep a close watch on the quality of Hallmark products until his death in 1982 at the age of ninety-one. Hall believed the secret to his success was that throughout his life, he demanded excellence—from himself and from those around him. He also believed that he succeeded in business because he simply worked harder than anyone else. Not surprising for a man who asked millions of people to "care enough to send the very best."

For More Information

Books

Hall, Joyce C. *When You Care Enough*. Kansas City, MO: Hallmark Cards, 1993.

Periodicals

Andrews, Kelly J. "Outsourcing Lessons From Hallmark." *Target Marketing* (December 1999): p. 22.

Cyr, Diane. "The Crown Rests on Royalty." *Direct* (April 15, 1996): pp. 1–5.

Ebeling, Ashlea. "Wild Card." *Forbes* (November 13, 2000): pp. 250.

Gilbert, Jennifer. "Family Rule Restored at Hallmark." *Chief Executive* (December 2001): pp. 14–15.

Matthes, Karen. "Greetings From Hallmark." *HR Focus* (August 1993): pp. 12–14.

"Roses Are Red, Card Sellers Blue: Buffeted by Technology and Demography, Greeting-Card Companies Struggle With the Medium and the Message." *Time* (April 19, 1999): p. 34.

Web Sites

Crayola Crayons [On-line] http://www.crayola.com (accessed on August 15, 2002).

Hallmark Cards, Inc. [On-line] http://www.hallmark.com (accessed on August 15, 2002).

Harpo, Inc.

110 North Carpenter Street
Chicago, IL 60607
(312) 633-0808
www.oprah.com

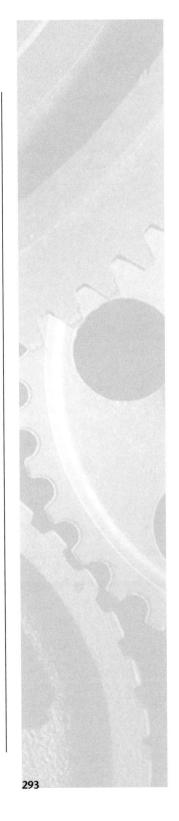

Harpo, Inc. is a privately held company owned by talk-show superstar Oprah Winfrey and her longtime lawyer, Jeff Jacobs. The backbone of the company, however, is Winfrey, who is one of the most celebrated personalities in the world. Harpo, which is Oprah spelled backwards, is really an extension of Winfrey the person. Its projects reflect her tastes and her desire to bring a measure of control and spirituality to her life. With Harpo, Inc., Winfrey used her popularity on television to expand into movie production and publishing, making her the most successful African American business owner in the United States, and one of the wealthiest entertainers in the world.

First Chicago, Then the Nation

The roots of Harpo can be traced to 1983, when Winfrey moved to Chicago, Illinois. After hosting a local talk show in Baltimore, Maryland, for several years, she began hosting *A.M. Chicago* on WLS-TV. Winfrey went head-to-head with the reigning king of morning talk shows, Phil Donahue (1935–). Also based in Chicago, Donahue reached a national audience

Harpo at a Glance

- **Employees:** 220

- **CEO:** Oprah Winfrey

- **Major Competitors:** Lifetime; WE Network; USA Networks; AOL Time Warner

- **Notable Projects:** *The Oprah Winfrey Show*; *O, the Oprah Magazine*; Oxygen Media; Oprah.com; Movies: *The Women of Brewster Place, The Wedding, Before Women Had Wings, Tuesdays with Morrie*

through syndication. This means that although his show was produced in Chicago, it was sold to other television stations across the country. Although Donahue was well known, Winfrey immediately clicked with Chicago viewers. Within a month, her ratings beat Donahue's in the region.

In 1984, Winfrey's agent negotiated a new deal with WLS that gave her an annual raise of $30,000 for the next four years. Winfrey, however, was not comfortable with the agent. She fired him and hired attorney Jeff Jacobs to represent her. "I'd heard Jeff is a piranha," she told *Forbes* in 1995. "I like that. Piranha is good." Jacobs's first important move was to get control of Winfrey's show from WLS. WLS, owned by the ABC network, had the syndication rights, and TV networks were not allowed to syndicate shows. This means that Winfrey's program would be stuck in the Chicago market. Jacobs convinced the network to give Winfrey the rights. ABC agreed, as long as ABC stations in other cities were given first shot at airing the program.

Jacobs changed the name of the program to *The Oprah Winfrey Show* and worked out a deal with King World Productions for syndication. King World already syndicated the popular game shows *Wheel of Fortune* and *Jeopardy!* In 1986, *The Oprah Winfrey Show* first appeared nationally, and Winfrey proved as popular across the country as she had been in Chicago. Her show earned $115 million during its first two years of syndication, with Winfrey getting a share of the profits.

From Oprah to Harpo

In 1986, Oprah set up Harpo Productions, Inc, making herself chairwoman. She gave Jacobs 5 percent ownership in the company (his share rose to 10 percent when he became company president in 1989). In 1987, Jacobs shut down his private law practice to devote himself to Harpo full-time. His next

Timeline

1983: Oprah Winfrey moves to Chicago to become the host of *A.M. Chicago.*

1984: Winfrey hires attorney Jeff Jacobs as her agent and business manager.

1985: *A.M. Chicago* become *The Oprah Winfrey Show* as Jacobs plans to syndicate it.

1986: Winfrey forms Harpo Productions, Inc.

1988: Harpo buys a film studio in Chicago.

1989: Harpo Productions releases the TV movie, *The Women of Brewster Place.*

1995: Harpo signs a deal with ABC to produce six made-for-TV movies.

1996: Winfrey introduces a monthly book club on her show, dramatically boosting sales for her featured books.

1998: Winfrey becomes a partner in Oxygen, a new cable TV network aimed at women.

2000: The first issue of *O, the Oprah Magazine* hits newsstands.

2002: Winfrey announces her plan to stop producing her show in 2006.

big move for the company was making Winfrey the owner of her show. He struck that deal with ABC and King World in July 1988, giving Winfrey the freedom to schedule and program the show as she chose.

Right after closing the deal, Winfrey bought a film production studio in Chicago. She planned to broadcast her show from there and to use the studio for other projects. George Mair, author of *Oprah: The Real Story,* quotes Winfrey's explanation for buying the studio: "I did this to really expand into the areas I wanted to and take over the show to create more time for me to do features and TV specials."

Winfrey's desire to expand into film and television was fueled by her successful acting debut in *The Color Purple* (1985). She was especially interested in projects relating to African American characters and issues. In 1989, Harpo Productions made the TV movie *The Women of Brewster Place,* with Winfrey in one of the lead roles. Reviews of the film were mixed, but

Oprah Winfrey made her debut on the big screen in _The Color Purple_ in 1985.
Reproduced by permission of The Kobal Collection.

ratings were high, and the next year, Winfrey produced a TV series based on the movie. _Brewster Place_ was the first show filmed in the new Harpo Studios. The show, however, was not as popular as the movie and ABC quickly cancelled it, although the network continued to broadcast films produced by Harpo. ABC also aired an hour-long interview Winfrey conducted in 1993 with singer Michael Jackson (1958–).

New Direction, New Projects

By 1993, Winfrey was worth an estimated $250 million. And, like only a handful of celebrities, she was so famous that she was known by just her first name. Regardless, Winfrey did not escape criticism. Even though her talk show was number one in the country, the segments often featured sensational topics and guests, such as devil worship and members of racial hate groups. One critic was Vicki Abt, a professor of sociology.

In 1994, Abt attacked Winfrey and other talk-show hosts for featuring trashy topics. The professor met with Winfrey and made suggestions for improving her content. The same year, Winfrey's show began to take on a more positive, uplifting tone. In 1995, she told *Ebony* she was disgusted with talk shows that "are designed to appeal to the lowest sense of ourselves, the bottom of what people experience." At first, Winfrey's ratings fell a bit with her new format, but they soon recovered. By 1998, her show reached about fifteen million viewers every day and was broadcast in dozens of countries around the world.

Oprah Winfrey spent $20 million to buy and renovate the space that would eventually become Harpo Studios. The studio covers 88,000 square feet and features three separate sound stages. Sound stages are areas where movies and television shows are filmed. The development of Harpo Studios made Winfrey just the third American woman ever to own her own studio.

Harpo Productions continued its work with ABC, signing a deal in 1995 to produce six made-for-TV movies. The company also remained interested in producing films for theater release. Its first feature film, *Beloved,* was released in 1998 by the **Walt Disney Company** (see entry). Based on a novel by Nobel Prize-winner Toni Morrison (1931–), the movie featured Winfrey, but it was not a hit with the public. Harpo had better luck with two TV films released during the 1997–98 season, *Before Women Had Wings* and *The Wedding.* The movies had high ratings and won praise from critics. Harpo Productions had one of its biggest hits ever in 2000 with the made-for-TV movie *Tuesdays With Morrie.* Featuring acclaimed actor Jack Lemmon (1925–2001), the movie won four Emmy Awards, television's highest honor.

Still, Winfrey's success came primarily from her daily show, as she proved in 1996 with the introduction of Oprah's Book Club. Once a month, Winfrey selected a book she enjoyed, and featured the author on her show. After a show aired, sales for a Winfrey pick skyrocketed, often by as much as one million copies. Winfrey ended the book club in 2002, disappointing many authors and publishers, but she promised to promote worthy books as she discovered them.

Winfrey continued branching out into new media in 1998. Harpo Productions, along with ABC Internet Group,

Beefing about Winfrey and Harpo

Although Oprah Winfrey has millions of fans, not everyone has had kind words for her or her show. In 1994, a former employee quit Harpo, Inc., and sued the company for back pay. She claimed she left Harpo because of the "environment of dishonesty and chaos." Winfrey settled the suit out of court two years later, and today all Harpo employees sign a statement promising never to speak publicly about Winfrey or her company.

In 1998, Winfrey was involved in a very public court case. On a 1996 show that examined how cattle are raised and the possibilities of getting "mad cow disease" from tainted beef, Winfrey said she would never eat another hamburger. Soon after, prices for cattle began to fall, and several Texas cattle ranchers sued her under the False Disparagement of Perishable Foods Products Act. This Texas law prohibits making false statements about food produced in the state, if the statements hurt business. Some people noted that cattle prices were already falling before Winfrey's comment, but the case went to trial in Amarillo, Texas, in January 1998.

Instead of avoiding publicity over the lawsuit, Winfrey moved her show to Amarillo for the length of the trial. On her shows there, she praised Texas culture and won the support of the local citizens. In court, she defended the fact that she and her guests had the right to speak their minds. According to *Texas Monthly,* she testified: "I provide a forum for people to express their opinions.... We are allowed to do this in the United States of America." Winfrey won the case, defeating the cattlemen on their own turf.

launched Oprah.com. The Web site let viewers of Winfrey's show keep track of recent book club selections, suggest topics for future shows, and share their thoughts on personal subjects. The same year, Harpo Group LLC joined with several partners to form Oxygen, a new cable channel dedicated to women and their issues, which also had its own Web site. Before Oxygen's debut in 2000, Winfrey told *Newsweek* her goals for the network. "If we can create on this network what we've been able to create on the 'Oprah' show, then we'll be highly successful." Harpo's first production for Oxygen was a twelve-part series featuring Winfrey helping women learn about the Internet.

O, More Success

Two months after Oxygen came on the air, Winfrey entered the publishing business with her own magazine *O, the Oprah Magazine*. After just seven issues, *O* had two million subscribers, making it the most successful new magazine in U.S. history. Although Winfrey worked with Hearst Magazines in producing *O*, she had complete control over its content. The magazine was a print version of her show, featuring interviews with celebrities and articles on how readers could find more meaning in their lives.

In 2002, Winfrey announced that was going to stop producing her show in 2006, although she had talked about quitting before and changed her mind. *O* also continued to make a substantial profit. Winfrey told *Fortune* that of all her accomplishments, she was most proud of her magazine "because I didn't know what I was doing." Oxygen, however, was struggling to gain viewers. In 2002, Winfrey cut a deal to do a new evening program for the network.

Winfrey, however, remains committed to television and finding new ways to help and entertain others. "I believe I'm just getting started," Winfrey said at a speech she gave in 2001. "If you're open to the possibilities, your life gets bigger, grander, bolder!"

Oprah Winfrey standing in front of the cover of the premiere issue of *O, the Oprah Magazine*. *O* debuted in April 1999.

Reproduced by permission of AP/Wide World Photos.

Oprah Winfrey.
Reproduced by permission of Archive Photos, Inc.

Oprah Winfrey

Born: January 29, 1954
Kosciusko, Mississippi
Talk-show host and founder, Harpo, Inc.

"Don't complain about what you don't have. Use what you've got. To do less than your best is a sin. Every single one of us has the power for greatness, because greatness is determined by service—to yourself and to others."

From an early age, Oprah Winfrey was comfortable in front of crowds. Her ease with audiences while simply being herself helped her become the most popular talk-show host in the United States. Winfrey, however, did more than explore hot topics and interview guests. She prodded her audience—dominated by women—to help others and find meaning in their lives. Through her show, her magazine O, and her public appearances, Winfrey emerged as a sort of preacher with an important message: "Live your best life."

While using her own "power for greatness" and helping others find theirs, Winfrey built a corporate empire, Harpo, Inc. Winfrey readily admits she is not much of a business woman. Instead, she relies on the skills of her executives and her own instincts. So far, those instincts have proven strong, as most of her projects have connected deeply with an audience that looks to her for information and inspiration.

Humble—and Painful—Beginnings

Winfrey, the wealthiest African American woman ever, faced hardship and personal problems before hitting the road to stardom. She was born on January 29, 1954, in Kosciusko, Mississippi, the product of a brief affair between teenager Vernita Lee and Vernon Winfrey, a twenty-year-old soldier. (Winfrey later acknowledged that she and her mother had no proof Vernon Winfrey was her biological father.) Baby Oprah was supposed to be Orpah, a name taken from the Bible, but a mix-up on her birth certificate made it Oprah.

While living with her father for the first time, at age eight, Oprah Winfrey amazed church audiences with her speaking skills. She also took notes on the minister's sermons, then gave her own version the next day on the school playground.

Winfrey and her mother spent several years living with Lee's parents on their farm. Like many poor, rural families of the era, the Lees had no indoor plumbing, and the family wore homemade clothes. After several years, Winfrey's mother left her daughter with the grandparents to live in Milwaukee, Wisconsin. Winfrey's grandmother taught her to read before she was three. Winfrey also began speaking at the family church, reciting sermons. Adults loved the smart and assured young girl. Other children, however, taunted her.

At age six, Winfrey went to live with her mother in Milwaukee. Except for one year when she lived with her father in Nashville, Tennessee, Winfrey stayed in Milwaukee for the next eight years. During that time, Winfrey was sexually abused by male relatives and their friends. At fourteen, she had a premature baby that died after birth. Winfrey kept her teen pregnancy a secret for many years. Her half-sister Patricia went public with the story in 1990. At the time, Vernita Lee was on welfare and unable to control her daughter. She tried to put Winfrey in a home for troubled teenaged girls. The home was full, so Winfrey returned to Nashville to live with her father.

From Beauty Queen to Television Host

Her second stay in Nashville changed Winfrey's life for the better. Her father and stepmother Zelma were respected members of Nashville's black community, and they gave her both discipline and love. Winfrey became active in the church and excelled in school. She also entered and won several local beauty contests. In 1971, she was named Miss Black Tennessee. The same year, she got a job reading the news part-time at

In 1987, Winfrey won her first Emmy Award as a talk-show host; her program won the Emmy for Best Daytime Talk Show. By 2002, she and *The Oprah Winfrey Show* had won more than thirty Emmys. Winfrey's other honors include a Lifetime Achievement Award from the National Academy of Television Arts & Sciences and a gold medal from the National Book Foundation, for her efforts to promote reading.

WVOL, a local radio station. Winfrey kept the job when she entered Tennessee State University, where she majored in drama and speech.

In 1973, while still at Tennessee State, Winfrey moved to TV news, working for WVTF. She was the station's first African American female woman anchor. Winfrey left college to pursue TV news full time, although she completed her course work years later to receive her degree. After three years at WVTF, Winfrey moved to WJZ in Baltimore, Maryland. For the first time in her young career, she failed. The casual, warm tone that she used in Nashville did not fit with her new station's more "professional" approach to the news. Winfrey was removed as the evening news co-anchor in April 1977 and ended up as the co-host of a morning talk show, *People Are Talking*. She later told *Time* that, "The minute the first show was over I thought, 'Thank God, I've found what I was meant to do.'"

Locally, *People are Talking* began to draw more viewers than the nationally syndicated *Phil Donahue Show*. WJZ tried syndicating the show, but only about a dozen stations agreed to air it. Winfrey, meanwhile, developed the style that would make her the top talk-show host in the country. She asked questions that explored her guests' deepest feelings, and viewers saw her as someone they could trust—a good friend who came into their homes on a TV screen.

In 1983, Winfrey left Baltimore to take over the morning talk show on WLS in Chicago—the program that became *The Oprah Winfrey Show*. Her rapid success in the new market led to another syndication deal. This time, Winfrey and her show were a hit across the country. Her role in the 1985 movie *The Color Purple* boosted her recognition. In 1986, Winfrey appeared in the film *Native Son*. That same year she also formed Harpo Productions, to take a more active role in television and film production. But no matter how many other projects she launched, Winfrey was best-loved for her talk show.

A Public Personal Life

Within a few years of starting her daily show, Winfrey was famous for talking about her personal struggles and successes on television. She always felt she was overweight, so in 1989 she went on a liquid diet and lost sixty-seven pounds. Winfrey then wheeled a cart-load of animal fat onto the stage of her show, representing the weight she had lost. In future years, her fans followed her constant struggle to lose the weight she eventually regained. On a more emotional level, Oprah used her show in 1991 to reveal her past sexual abuse. In a later show, she talked about using drugs to try to satisfy an old boyfriend. Her current love life also made headlines, as tabloid newspapers reported on her relationship with Stedman Graham, a Chicago educator. The two met in 1986 and have lived together for many years.

After revealing that she suffered abuse as a child, Oprah Winfrey led the effort to pass a new national law designed to keep track of convicted child abusers. Officially known as the National Child Protection Act, it was nicknamed the Oprah Bill. The law went into effect in 1993.

Winfrey used her interviewing skills and personal warmth to draw out painful information from guests who appeared on her program. Some newspapers and magazines talked about the "Oprahfication" of America—the tendency to use talk shows as a form of therapy for guests and the studio audience. Not everyone welcomed the trend, especially if the topics were sexual. By the mid 1990s, Winfrey decided to move away from the more questionable topics, and begin focusing on the positive qualities in people and her own life. Her show began to take on a more religious or spiritual feel. In 2002, she told *Fortune* her show was not just a product, "It's my soul. It's who I am."

With her strengthened desire to be a positive influence, Winfrey started her book club in 1996. The next year, she began "Oprah's Angel Network," which asked viewers to donate their spare change to worthy causes, such as education and build-ing homes for the poor. Winfrey's vast wealth also let her make generous contributions to different organizations. She donated millions of dollars to several African American universities.

Winfrey's more spiritual efforts, however, drew some criticism. In 2001, Oprah launched a speaking tour that encour-aged audiences to look within themselves for answers to life's

The Appeal of "Dr. Phil"

A married couple struggles to restore their happiness. A parent looks for ways to control a difficult teen. These are typical problems guests have brought to the *Oprah Winfrey Show,* and the man they turn to for help is Dr. Phil McGraw. Known on the show as "Dr. Phil" and "Dr. Tell It Like It Is," McGraw first appeared on Winfrey's show in 1998. The therapist's straightforward approach proved so popular, Winfrey made him a weekly guest. Thanks to his exposure on the show, McGraw has become one of the most famous psychologists in the United States. His three books have become best-sellers, and his talks often draw several thousand people.

Born in 1950, McGraw spent most of his childhood in Oklahoma before settling in Texas. He gave up a private practice to start his own company as a legal consultant. McGraw met Winfrey in 1997, when he helped her prepare for her trial after being sued by Texas cattlemen. On Winfrey's show, McGraw offered what the host called "Philisms"—short, direct sayings that cut to the heart of a problem. A typical Philism, as reported in the *Palm Beach Post*: "Make a decision and pull the trigger."

McGraw's popularity has led to another business opportunity for Winfrey's Harpo, Inc. In 2001, the company announced it would produce McGraw's own syndicated talk show, starting in the fall of 2002. Within months, King World Productions announced that *Dr. Phil* had been sold to more than one hundred stations that reach about 85 percent of the country's TV viewers.

questions, while also having faith in God or some higher power. *People* reported the reaction of noted writer Barbara Grizutti Harrison to Winfrey's approach: "She thinks she's the messiah, leading everyone to the promised land." Still, Winfrey's devoted fans admired the way she inspired others. Mary Madden, a New York housewife, told *Newsweek* in 2001, "She's giving me the tools to find myself."

Winfrey's fame and spiritual outlook made her a logical choice to serve as host for a prayer service to honor New York's victims of the September 11, 2001, terrorist attacks. With religious leaders of many faiths by her side, Winfrey expressed one of the common themes in her shows and in her life: "May we leave this place determined to ... create deeper meaning, to know what really matters."

For More Information

Books

Lowe, Janet. *Oprah Winfrey Speaks.* New York: John Wiley & Sons, 1998.

Mair, George. *Oprah Winfrey: The Real Story.* Rev. ed. Secaucus, NJ: Citadel Stars, 1998.

In 2002, Harpo, Inc. was worth an estimated $575 million. Winfrey's other business deals and investments gave her a total worth just under $1 billion. Her personal holdings included a 160-acre farm in Indiana and a California mansion worth $51 million.

Periodicals

Cheakalos, Christina. "Direct Males." *People* (June 11, 2001): p. 89.

Clemetson, Lynette. "Talk Show: 'Oxygen Gives Me That Voice.'" *Newsweek* (November 15, 1999): p. 64.

Farley, Christopher John. "Queen of All Media." *Time* (October 5, 1998): p. 82.

Folstad, Kim. "Dr. Phil: Buy the Book." *Palm Beach Post* (March 6, 2002): p. 1D.

Hollandsworth, Skip, and Pamela Colloff. "How the West Was Won Over." *Texas Monthly* (March 1998): p. 100.

La Franco, Robert, and Josh McHugh. "'Piranha is Good.'" *Forbes* (October 16, 1995): p. 66.

Oldenburg, Ann. "Dr. Phil's Advice: Wake Up!" *USA Today* (May 8, 2001): p. 1D.

"Oprah on Oprah." *Newsweek* (January 8, 2001): p. 38.

Randolph, Laura B. "Oprah!" *Ebony* (July 1995): p. 22.

——. "Oprah Opens up About Her Weight, Her Wedding, and Why She Withheld the Book." *Ebony* (October 1993): p. 130.

Sellers, Patricia. "The Business of Being Oprah." *Fortune* (April 1, 2002): p. 50.

Smolowe, Jill, and Sonja Steptoe. "O on the Go." *People* (July 16, 2001): p. 50.

Web Sites

Oprah.com [On-line] http://www.oprah.com (accessed on August 15, 2002).

Oxygen. [On-line] http://www.oxygen.com (accessed on August 15, 2002).

Hershey Foods Corporation

100 Crystal A Drive
Hershey, PA 17033
(717) 534-6799
www.hersheys.com

Hershey Foods Corporation headquarters, Hershey, Pennsylvania.
Reproduced by permission of Corbis Corporation (Bellevue).

For many Americans, the word *chocolate* makes them think of Hershey's. Milton Hershey, the founder of the Hershey Foods Corporation, made his first milk chocolate bar an affordable treat customers could buy almost anywhere. Today, Hershey's chocolate comes in all forms, from bite-size "kisses" to chocolate syrup and chocolate milk. Hershey Foods, however, is more than just chocolate. By purchasing other companies Hershey expanded and now sells gum, licorice, breath mints, and hard candy, with many of its products marketed around the world. In the Unites States, Hershey has become the country's leading chocolate and candy maker.

From Caramel to Chocolate

Milton Hershey spent many years trying to succeed in the candy business before he perfected the milk chocolate bar. As a teenager, he worked with a confectioner (candy maker) in Lancaster, Pennsylvania, not far from his hometown of Derry Church. In 1876, Hershey opened his own candy business in Philadelphia, but that and several other efforts in other cities failed. Finally, in 1886, he opened the Lancaster Caramel Company, making the chewy candy with milk, unlike most confectioners of the time. Hershey's "Crystal A" caramels were an immediate hit.

For some of his caramels, Hershey added a bit of cocoa powder, which came from the same beans used to make cocoa butter, the main ingredient in chocolate. In 1893, Hershey watched a German manufacturer of chocolate-making equipment produce chocolate bars. He bought the same machinery for his company to make chocolate coatings for his caramels. Soon, however, he decided to sell chocolate and cocoa as separate products. The next year, the Hershey Chocolate Company started as a division of the Lancaster Caramel Company.

To sell his new candies, Hershey hired William Murrie. To advertise the products, he bought an electric car—one of the first in Pennsylvania—and painted "Hershey's Cocoa" on each side. Hershey not only made plain bars, he also molded his chocolate to look like cigars, miniature bicycles, and many other items. By 1900, he decided to get out of the caramel business and devote himself to chocolate. Hershey sold the Lancaster Caramel Company for $1 million and kept the Hershey Chocolate Company. He also began plans to build a new factory.

Hershey at a Glance

- **Employees:** 14,300
- **CEO:** R. H. Lenny
- **Subsidiaries:** Hershey Chocolate & Confectionery Corporation; Hershey Chocolate of Virginia
- **Major Competitors:** Mars, Inc.; Nestlé; Russell Stover Candies, Inc.; William Wrigley Jr. Company; Tootsie Roll Industries
- **Notable Products:** Hershey's chocolate bar; Hershey's Kisses; Reese's Pieces; York Peppermint Patties; Twizzler's Licorice; Hershey's syrup; Hershey's cocoa; Jolly Rancher Fruit Chews; Reese's NutRageous; Skor bar

Chocolate for Everyone

For several years, Hershey made chocolate out of a rented factory while he looked for the land for his new plant. Finally, he chose a site in Derry Church. The area had many dairy farms, which was handy since Hershey needed fresh milk to make his milk chocolate. Adding milk to chocolate gave it a light color and smooth taste. The process had been

Timeline

1894: Candy maker Milton Hershey sells his first milk chocolate bars.

1905: The Hershey Chocolate Company opens its first factory in the town of Hershey, Pennsylvania.

1918: Milton Hershey donates most of his wealth to the trust that runs the Hershey Industrial School for orphaned boys.

1931: Annual sales at Hershey reach $31 million.

1945: Milton Hershey dies.

1963: Hershey buys the H. B. Reese Candy Company.

1968: Hershey changes its name to the Hershey Foods Corporation.

1970: Hershey runs national advertising for the first time.

1988: Hershey buys Peter Paul/Cadbury candies.

2001: Hershey announces record quarterly sales.

discovered in Europe in 1875, but Hershey spent several years developing his own recipe for milk chocolate. When his factory opened in 1905, Hershey concentrated on selling chocolate bars at five cents each.

At the time, most Americans had never tasted either milk or dark chocolate. Chocolate was expensive and sold only at candy shops or in drugstores. Hershey believed everyone should be able to afford chocolate, and they should be able to buy it anywhere. Joël Glenn Brenner, author of *The Emperors of Chocolate,* quotes Hershey as saying, "It is more than a sweet, it is a food." By producing huge numbers of chocolate bars, Hershey kept his prices low. He also convinced grocery stores, newsstands, diners, and other businesses to carry his bars. Then, unlike most chocolate makers, Hershey sold his bars across the United States, not just in one region.

Directly around his plant Hershey built a new town, with homes for his workers. The town of Hershey grew to include a school, stores, an amusement park, and a zoo. Hershey provided the heat, water, and electricity to the town's residents, and no one paid taxes. In 1909, Hershey and his wife Catherine opened the Hershey Industrial School, which educated orphaned boys. With his town and school, Hershey became known as one of America's most generous businessmen.

The success of Hershey's chocolate bars fed that generosity. So did a new product introduced in 1907: Hershey's Kisses. By 1911, annual sales at the company reached $5 million. Hershey was not involved in most daily operations, leaving that to Murrie, his first salesman and close friend. After November 1918, Hershey did not even own the company bearing his name. When his wife died, he gave his estate to the Hershey Trust, which had been set up to run the Industrial School. The Hershey Company sold shares to the public starting in 1927, but the trust remained the principal owner.

> When it opened in 1905, the Hershey plant was the most modern candy factory in the world. By 1915, the company was producing more than 100,000 pounds of chocolate every day. The plant remains the world's largest chocolate factory.

More Products, New Companies

The Hershey company introduced several new chocolate candies during the 1920s and 1930s. First was Mr. Goodbar in 1925, a chocolate bar with peanuts. Krackel, chocolate and crisped rice, hit store shelves in 1938, and Hershey Miniatures appeared the next year. The company also provided the raw chocolate used by other confectioners for their candies. Sales grew even as the United States struggled through the Great Depression of the 1930s, the economic downturn that threw millions of people out of work and left many hungry and homeless.

The Depression stirred some industrial workers who did have jobs to form unions. The unions tried to win higher pay and better working conditions for workers. Strikes and violence broke out at some factories, including Hershey's. Workers closed the plant and demanded the company let them join a national union. The strike ended several days later when area dairy farmers, angered because they were losing money as the factory sat

Chocolate goes through many different stages of processing before it is packaged and sold.
Reproduced by permission of Corbis Corporation (Bellevue).

idle, attacked the strikers. Hershey eventually agreed to let the workers unionize.

More changes followed in the 1940s. Hershey died in 1945, and Murrie retired two years later. By then, the Hershey Chocolate Company controlled 90 percent of the milk chocolate market in the United States. During the 1950s, however, the company seemed to lack direction. Competition increased, and companies in Europe were streamlining their production with new equipment. Hershey also did not advertise, following the long-held belief of Milton Hershey: "Quality is the best kind of advertising."

The company finally began to modernize in the early 1960s, under the leadership of Samuel Hinkle. Hinkle added new equipment to speed up production and opened Hershey's first foreign plant in Canada. In 1963, Hershey grew with its purchase of the H. B. Reese Candy Company, famous for its chocolate-and-peanut butter cups. The company also moved beyond candy in 1966, with the purchase of pasta makers San Giorgio and Delmonico Foods. To reflect its new products, the company changed its name in 1968 to Hershey Foods Corporation. Two years later, Hershey advertised for the first time, placing ads in newspapers and broadcasting ads nationally on radio and television.

Rivalry with Mars

The advertising was a response to Hershey's slipping sales, primarily to its major U.S. competitor, Mars, Inc. Advertising and marketing increased under William Dearden, who took over as chief executive officer (CEO) in 1976. Dearden also continued to move the company beyond chocolate manufacturing. By 1979, Hershey had bought several more pasta companies, the largest U.S. licorice manufacturer, and Friendly's, a chain of family restaurants that specialized in ice cream. (Hershey sold Friendly's in 1988). By 1982, about 30 percent of Hershey's $1.5 billion in sales came from non-candy products.

In 1982, Hershey Foods scored a major victory in its chocolate "war" with Mars. The competitor turned down a chance to have its M&M candies featured in a new movie by director **Steven Spielberg** (see **Dreamworks SKG** entry). Hershey's, however, jumped at the opportunity to promote a relatively new product, Reese's Pieces. The movie was *E.T.: The Extra-Terrestrial*, which became one of the most popular films ever. One Hershey executive said in *The Emperors of Chocolate*, "It was the biggest marketing coup in history.... We got immediate recognition for our product, the kind of recognition we would normally have to pay fifteen or twenty million bucks for."

Hershey's Miniatures, first made and sold in 1939, have been popular ever since.
Reproduced by permission of AP/Wide World Photos.

The success of Reese's Pieces and several other new products, plus the 1988 purchase of the U.S. interests of British candy maker Cadbury Schweppes PLC, helped Hershey regain its spot as the top American candy company. Hershey also expanded its presence in Europe, buying a plant from a German company in 1991.

Fighting to Stay on Top

Since the early 1990s, Hershey has continued to battle Mars for the top spot in chocolate manufacturing. It has introduced successful new products, such as Hershey's Hugs (Kisses made from white chocolate) and Reese's NutRageous bar. The company has also bought other candy companies, including Leaf North America, the maker of Jolly Rancher hard candies. And Hershey's has sometimes worked with other companies to market products with the Hershey name.

Hershey Goes to War

During World War II (1939–45), Hershey played an important role in giving U.S. soldiers the energy they needed on the battlefield. After World War I (1914–18), the company worked with U.S. officials to design a chocolate-based bar loaded with nutrition and calories. The end result was the Field Ration D, a bar that mixed oat flour and vitamins with chocolate. Unlike regular chocolate, the new bar would stay solid at up to 120 degrees Fahrenheit, and inside its special packaging it stayed dry for up to an hour when placed in water. Hershey's made more than one billion of these rations, and U.S. soldiers carried the Hershey name all over the world. The military continued to use the Field Ration D until the 1970s.

Hershey chocolate went to war again in 1990, as U.S. soldiers prepared to fight in the Persian Gulf War (1991). Hershey developed a chocolate bar that would stay solid at temperatures up to 140 degrees Fahrenheit—perfect for the hot desert climate of the Persian Gulf area. Unlike the World War II bars, however, these "Desert Bars" tasted just like a regular Hershey bar. The company sent almost a million Desert Bars overseas and also sold them at home.

In 2001, an economic downturn hurt sales in many industries. Hershey, however, announced record sales in the third quarter of that year, a little more than $1.3 billion. Still, the company announced job layoffs and the closing of several plants. Hershey's and other chocolate makers also faced bad publicity that year. Several newspapers reported that some of the raw cocoa used to make chocolate is picked and processed by children held as slaves on farms in several African nations. In November 2001, Hershey and other U.S. chocolate companies announced they would start a program to eliminate the abuses.

Despite its problems, the Hershey Foods Corporation remains on top in the chocolate and candy industry. It continues to expand its efforts overseas and roll out new products designed to tempt the sweet tooth of candy buyers everywhere.

Milton Hershey

Born: September 13, 1857
Derry Church, Pennsylvania
Died: October 13, 1945
Hershey, Pennsylvania
Founder, Hershey Foods Corporation

Milton Hershey.
*Reproduced by permission of
Corbis Corporation.*

For the first part of his career, Milton Hershey struggled to succeed in the candy business. Despite his early failures, he never gave up. Hershey's fame finally came as the first American manufacturer of milk chocolate. Using the most modern methods of production available, Hershey developed, as his slogan once said, "the Great American Chocolate Bar."

On the Move

Money was not plentiful for young Milton Snavely Hershey and his family. He was born on September 13, 1857, in Derry Church (sometimes called Derry Township), Pennsylvania. His parents Henry and Fanny were Mennonites, a small group of Protestants who lived simply and opposed violence in any form. Mennonites from Germany and Switzerland had started settling in central Pennsylvania in the 1680s. Most were farmers. Henry Hershey, however, was drawn to business, and he started more than a dozen ventures, including drilling for oil. These businesses, however, always failed, leaving the Hersheys scrambling for income.

"We were starting out to do something new, something that had never been done before.... We had to learn by doing things, and when we did them right, we did more of it that way. And what we did wrong, well, you had to remember that, too, so you wouldn't keep making the same mistakes over and over."

Milton Hershey was generous with his wealth, but some people still saw him as cheap or a harsh employer. He sometimes snuck up on workers, trying to catch them sneaking a break on the job. He also refused to spend money on advertising. One story says that when he saw Hershey chocolate-bar wrappers thrown on the ground as garbage, he turned them over so the name showed—a form of free advertising.

Henry Hershey's different projects kept his family moving from town to town, disrupting his son's education. He never went beyond fourth grade. When the young Hershey was fourteen, his mother arranged for him to become an apprentice to a printer. As an apprentice, Hershey's job was to help his "master" and learn the trade. After just three months, Hershey was fired.

In 1872, Hershey tried a second apprenticeship with a confectioner based in nearby Lancaster. This job went better, and in 1876 Hershey had enough skills to enter the candy business on his own. Borrowing money from relatives, he moved to Philadelphia and started making taffy and caramel, selling the candy from a pushcart. The business lasted six years, but a partnership with his father ate away Hershey's profits. Hershey left Philadelphia in 1882 after suffering a mental breakdown that kept him in bed for weeks.

After his recovery, Hershey followed his father west, to Colorado. He took a job at a confectioner's making caramel. On the job, Hershey learned how to improve the candy's taste by adding fresh milk. From Denver, Hershey moved to Chicago and New Orleans, Louisiana, before settling in New York City. He worked for a confectioner and made his own caramels on the side, using the recipe he discovered in Colorado. He eventually started his own candy company. The company failed, as Hershey tried to grow too quickly.

The Chocolate Town

Returning to Lancaster, Pennsylvania, Hershey once again borrowed money, this time from Harry Lebkicher, who had worked for him in Pennsylvania. Later, his mother and her family helped as well, and in 1886 Hershey formed the Lancaster Caramel Company. The company grew quickly, and Hershey was soon rich. In his biography of Hershey, *One of a Kind,* Charles Schuyler Castner writes that Hershey told one business

Lifelong Member of the Hershey "Family"

After his mother died in 1935, thirteen-year-old William Dearden of Philadelphia was sent to the Hershey Industrial School. Dearden learned that in many ways, the boys at the Hershey school lived better than millions of American children of the era. They received three meals every day and wore new clothes. Outside of class, the boys took trips to concerts, theatres, and the movies. In return, they helped run the school, working on its farm and cleaning the buildings. Looking in on them throughout their stay was Milton Hershey.

Only a few graduates of the Hershey Industrial School stayed to work at the Hershey Chocolate Company. Just one—William Dearden—worked his way up and eventually ran the company. After graduating high school, Dearden spent one year at a junior college funded by the Hershey Trust, then went to Albright College, in Reading, Pennsylvania. During World War II (1939–45), he spent one year at the Harvard Business School before joining the U.S. Navy as a supply officer. After the war, he worked in New Jersey, returned to military service during the Korean War (1950–53), then came back to Hershey to work at the school where he had spent his teenage years.

Dearden began working at the chocolate company in 1957, serving as an assistant to the chairman, John J. Gallagher. In 1965, he took the newly created position of director of sales and marketing. Dearden led Hershey's first efforts to actively promote the company's products. In 1976, he was named chief executive officer (CEO) of the company. Despite his success, Dearden never forgot his roots or lost touch with workers and employees.

When Dearden stepped down as CEO of Hershey in 1985, the company had regained some of the ground it had lost to Mars, Inc., during the 1970s. To Dearden, strengthening the company was his way of repaying Milton Hershey. In an oral history about his life, Dearden said, "I felt I owed Mr. Hershey for what he did for me as a boy."

associate, "One day I looked at the books, and there … was over a hundred thousand dollars in the bank, and I didn't owe any of it."

As the Lancaster Caramel Company grew, Hershey turned his attention to other foods. In 1892, he visited Switzerland, hoping to learn how to make cheese. On the trip, he discovered milk chocolate. The next year, Hershey bought equipment to make chocolate and began selling it along with his caramels. Perfecting his own milk chocolate, however, took several more years.

In his later food experiments, Milton Hershey made sherbet out of such vegetables as beets and onions. He also invented an ice cream that did not contain milk. Made mostly from rice flour, peanut oil, and sugar, this non-dairy ice cream was half the price of regular ice cream and came in chocolate, vanilla, and strawberry.

By 1900, Hershey was happily married to Catherine Sweeney. He and his wife enjoyed his riches from caramel, often traveling abroad. But Hershey was ready to try something new, and he sold his caramel business to devote himself to chocolate. Hershey did not necessarily want to increase his wealth. Instead, he planned to build his own town, where workers at his factory could make enough money to enjoy a good life. The idea struck his friends and family as odd. His wife, according to Joël Glenn Brenner in *The Emperors of Chocolate,* said her husband "ought to go have his head examined."

Hershey, however, was determined to build his own "Chocolate Town," on land he bought in his birthplace of Derry Church. He opened his chocolate factory in 1905. Work had already begun on the town, with Hershey planning neighborhoods and naming the main streets: Chocolate Avenue and Cocoa Avenue. Workers moved into the homes he built for them, and Hershey served as the town's fire chief, police officer, and mayor.

Life beyond Chocolate

In the factory, Hershey and his employees perfected their version of milk chocolate, then began selling it across the United States. Hershey's modern plant sped up the production of milk chocolate, which had previously been made by hand. Hershey put a long-time employee, William Murrie, in charge of the business, and he and his wife continued their travels. They also used their wealth to start the Hershey Industrial School for orphans. In a 1923 interview with the *New York Times,* Hershey explained why he founded the school: "I have no heirs; so I decided to make the orphan boys of the United States my heirs."

Hershey showed his commitment to "his" boys (girls were admitted later) in 1918. Three years after the death of his wife, Hershey gave almost his entire fortune to the trust that ran the school. Hershey, however, still worked closely with Murrie and others on how the company was run. During the Great Depression of the 1930s, Hershey hired hundreds of out-of-work Pennsylvania residents to construct new buildings in his town.

In 1937, on the night he celebrated his eightieth birthday, Hershey suffered a stroke. By some reports, he had only a few days to live, but Hershey recovered and kept busy looking for new crops to plant in Hershey and new candies to make and market. He kept an office in the Hershey plant and lived in two rooms at his former mansion, which he donated to the Hershey Country Club. Hershey also continued to travel, although he stayed close to Pennsylvania instead of traveling the world as he once did. Hershey remained active until his death in 1945. The company and town he founded continued to grow, the product of a man driven to give the world pleasure through chocolate.

For More Information

Books

Brenner, Joël Glenn. *The Emperors of Chocolate*. New York: Random House, 1999.

Castner, Charles Schuyler. *One of a Kind: Milton Snavely Hershey, 1857–1945*. Hershey, PA: The Derry Literary Guild, 1983.

Periodicals

Altman, Henry. "Hershey's 'New' Ingredient." *Nation's Business* (June 1983): p. 42.

"Hershey Foods to Close Some Plants and Cut Jobs." *The New York Times* (October 25, 2001): p. C4.

Novak, Janet. "The High-profit Candy Habit." *Forbes* (June 29, 1987): p. 76.

Wawro, Thaddeus. "The Candy Man." *Entrepreneur* (March 2000): p. 114.

Web Sites

Hershey Entertainment & Resorts Company. [On-line] http://www.hersheypa.com (accessed on August 15, 2002).

Hershey Foods Corporation. [On-line] http://www.hersheys.com (accessed on August 15, 2002).

Hershey Trust Company. [On-line] http://www.hersheytrust.org (accessed on August 15, 2002).

Hewlett-Packard Company

3000 Hanover Street
Palo Alto, CA 94304-1185
(650) 857-1501
www.hp.com

Hewlett-Packard Company headquarters, Palo Alto, California.
Reproduced by permission of AP/Wide World Photos.

Some of America's greatest cultural heroes are its basement inventors and self-made business owners. These people prove the claim that a good idea and hard work can lead to success. David Packard (1912–1996) and William "Bill" Hewlett (1913–2001) made their first product in a small garage. From there, they went on to build the world's second-largest computer manufacturing company.

For decades, Hewlett-Packard (HP) was also known for its loose management style, called "the HP Way." Packard and Hewlett never put themselves above their employees and gave them the freedom to try new ideas. In return, HP workers responded with commitment and loyalty. Those bonds, however, were tested in 2001, after Hewlett-Packard announced its merger with rival computer maker Compaq.

Building a Business

William Hewlett and David Packard met in 1930 as freshmen at Stanford University, in Palo Alto, California. They shared an interest in the outdoors and electrical engineering.

By their senior year, they were planning to form a radio company, an idea encouraged by Fred Terman, one of their professors. The business venture, however, was delayed for several years, as Hewlett earned a master's degree and Packard worked for **General Electric, Inc.** (GE; see entry) in New York. Finally, in the fall of 1938, Packard returned to California for graduate studies at Stanford, and he and Hewlett went to work.

Their first workshop was a one-car garage behind the two-family house they shared in Palo Alto. Their assets included a used drill press and a little more than $500. They made several electronic products, including an automatic toilet-bowl flusher for public restrooms. Writing in *American Heritage,* historian Frederick E. Allen quoted Hewlett as saying, "In the beginning, we did anything to bring in a nickel."

By November, the partners had built an audio oscillator, a device that creates high-frequency sounds. Their oscillator was cheaper and better than others on the market. They called their product the Model 200A, because, as Packard explains in his 1995 book, *The HP Way,* "We thought the name would make us look like we'd been around for a while." The partner's first major order came from the **Walt Disney Company** (see entry), which bought eight of the oscillators for $71.50 apiece. Since they were truly in business, Hewlett and Packard flipped a coin to see whose last name would go first in their new company's name.

Hewlett-Packard at a Glance

- **Employees:** 150,000

- **CEO:** Carleton Fiorina

- **Subsidiaries:** BT&D Technologies Ltd.; CoCreate Software GmbH; HP Computadores; Heartstream, Inc.; Microsensor Technology, Inc.; Technologies et Participations S.A.

- **Major Competitors:** International Business Machines (IBM); Dell Computer Corporation; Sun Microsystems, Inc.; Hitachi, Ltd.; Apple Computer, Inc.; Gateway, Inc.; Ingram Micro, Inc.

- **Notable Products:** LaserJet printer; DeskJet printer; OfficeJet printer/scanner/copier; Vectra desktop PC; Pavilion desktop PC; Pavilion portable PC; Omnibook portable PC; Jornada personal digital assistant (PDA)

Growth during War and Peace

After the United States entered World War II (1939–45) in 1941, HP's business grew. Hewlett served in the army, so Packard ran the company, which began building a variety of

Timeline

1939: David Packard and William Hewlett form Hewlett-Packard (HP) to sell the audio oscillator they invented.

1957: HP sells stock and drafts the company goals that form the heart of "The HP Way."

1966: HP Laboratories opens.

1968: An electronic desktop calculator is introduced.

1972: The first HP pocket calculator appears.

1984: HP introduces two new computer printers, the LaserJet and the DeskJet.

1991: HP sells a palmtop personal computer that weighs less than one pound.

1999: HP forms Agilent to develop and sell its testing and measuring.

2002: The purchase of Compaq Computer Corporation makes HP the second-largest computer manufacturer in the world.

electronic measuring and testing equipment for the U.S. government. By the end of the war, HP's annual sales reached $1 million, and the company had a new manufacturing plant and more than two hundred workers. HP introduced profit-sharing and a health insurance plan—benefits largely unheard of at the time. In profit-sharing each worker is given a bonus based on a company's sales.

A post-war downturn forced HP to fire some plant workers, but it hired more engineers, and in 1947 it formed a legal corporation. Within several years, the company was back up to two hundred employees and making a wide range of testing devices. By the end of the 1950s, HP had more than 350 products and was expanding into Europe.

The "HP Way" was also firmly in place. Hewlett and Packard believed in "management by walking around"—they spent much of their time talking to the engineers and other employees instead of tying themselves to a desk. At a 1957 management meeting, the company came up with six goals, later expanded to seven. As Packard wrote in *The HP Way,* the goals included giving employees "the opportunity to share in the company's success" and "striv[ing] for continual improvement in the quality, usefulness, and value of the products and services we offer customers."

That same year, 1957, Hewlett-Packard sold its first shares to the public. This means that shares, or small portions, of the company were available for sale on the New York Stock Exchange. The company also opened the first of six new buildings near Stanford University. In 1958, HP recorded sales of $30 million and had more than seventeen hundred workers.

In 1989, the garage where David Packard and William Hewlett began their business was named a California State Historical Landmark. The site was honored as the birthplace of "Silicon Valley," the state's center for high-tech manufacturing.

Calculating New Profits

During the 1960s, Hewlett-Packard grew by purchasing several smaller electronics firms and expanding beyond measurement and testing devices. HP introduced its first computer, the Model 2116, in 1966. It also did important work on light-emitting diodes (LED's), the small electronic lights now common on computers and other products. The company's most significant new item, however, was the world's first programmable scientific desktop calculator. Prior to this, calculators were noisy, mechanical machines that used gears. The HP Model 9100 was electronic, more like a computer than a calculator.

After the success of the 9100, Hewlett challenged his employees to build a calculator small enough to fit into a shirt pocket. The HP staff responded with the HP 35, which was an immediate hit with scientists and engineers. HP was the pioneer in powerful, handheld calculators, and it remained strong in the testing and measurement market. By 1980, annual sales were $3 billion, and the company had fifty-seven thousand employees.

Despite its size, HP kept a loose management structure. Each division in the company did its own research and development and manufactured its own products. As a division grew, it was split into smaller divisions. HP's increased movement into computers, however, presented the company with new structural and marketing challenges.

In 1966, Hewlett-Packard opened HP Labs, a new research facility. Today the company has seven research sites around the world, working on such products as computer storage systems, Internet technologies, and printers.

Printer Powerhouse

Although Hewlett-Packard had been making computers since the mid-1960s, it was not a major presence in the industry. HP began to address that in 1980, when it introduced its first personal computer (PC). It also produced larger, more powerful computers, some costing up to $25,000. The various HP models, however, were not compatible with each other. In addition, the company faced tough competition from International Business Machines (IBM), which had started selling personal computers in 1981. By the end of 1983, HP had less than five percent of the PC market. Still, the company knew its potential growth was tied to these smaller computers.

Although highly respected in technical circles, HP and its products were not well known by the average U.S. consumer. The company began a new advertising campaign to boost its image. HP also placed its different PC operations in one new group. Finally, in 1984, it introduced several new products. One was a portable computer that could work with IBM's popular PCs. Older HP models could not run IBM software. More significant were two new printers designed for any computer: the ThinkJet and the LaserJet.

The ThinkJet, an ink-jet printer, offered better print quality than other inexpensive printers on the market. The LaserJet came out of a partnership with Canon, a Japanese manufacturer of cameras and copiers. Priced at almost $3,500, the LaserJet was a high-quality business printer. In a 1984 interview with *Forbes*, Cyril Yansouni, the head of HP's new PC group, explained the printer's importance to the company: "If the LaserJet gets us into the executive office, they'll remember us the next time we come around with computers."

Over time, HP introduced new models of both printers, and prices fell while quality remained high. HP set the standard for computer printers and dominated the market. The sales of replacement ink and toner cartridges also helped boost profits. Over time, the company improved its PCs and slowly took over a larger part of that market.

Years of Change in the Computer Industry

By 1990, Hewlett-Packard's annual sales were more than $13 billion, but its profits were falling slightly. The company purchased Apollo Computer in 1989, and mixing its products and staff with HP's proved difficult. Thousands of jobs went unfilled after workers retired or left the company. To counter the slowing growth, the company began selling a new "palmtop" computer, the size of a pocket calculator with as much processing power as a PC. In 1992, it introduced a new color ink-jet printer, reinforcing its dominance in the printer market.

In 1976, Hewlett-Packard lost the opportunity to become a leader in the PC market when it decided not to develop a new personal computer built by one of its employees, Steve Wozniak. Wozniak left HP and co-founded **Apple Computer, Inc.** (see entry), the company credited with selling the first successful personal computer.

High-tech industries saw explosive growth during the 1990s, and HP benefited from this boom. Sales grew as much as $7 billion in one year. The company launched a new line of personal computers and continued to sell more sophisticated machines to businesses and researchers. By 1997, HP was the world's second-largest computer manufacturer with sales reaching $35.4 billion out of total company sales of $42.9 billion.

Despite its success with computers, HP faced tough competition and profits fell in 1998. The next year, it decided to concentrate on computers and related products. HP formed a new company, Agilent, to build and sell its testing and measuring devices. HP also made news in 1999 when it hired Carleton "Carly" Fiorina as chief executive officer (CEO). She was HP's first leader to come from outside the company.

Faced with slumping sales, Fiorina planned to increase HP's development of new products and combine its dozens of divisions into just three. A relationship with microchip maker Intel led to the Itanium, a new kind of chip for computers.

Fiorina's boldest move came in September 2001, when HP launched a takeover of rival Compaq Computer Corporation. Hewlett-Packard's decision to buy Compaq led to a long and public battle between Walter B. Hewlett (son of William Hewlett) and Fiorina. At first, Hewlett joined other board members in supporting the purchase, but by November 2001, he had

Two Hewlett-Packard
scientists stand next to a
scanning tunneling
microscope at the Hewlett-
Packard headquarters in
Palo Alto, California, that is
used as part of Hewlett-
Packard's molecular
electronics research.
*Reproduced by permission of
AP/Wide World Photos.*

announced his intention to vote against it. He controlled about 5 percent of HP's stock, owned by the Hewlett family and a foundation set up by his father, who had died earlier in the year.

As Hewlett spoke out against the deal, other shareholders and some employees questioned the move. Compaq's stock value fell during 2001, and some opponents claimed HP was paying too much for its rival. By December, Hewlett said that shareholders controlling almost 20 percent of HP's stock were against the deal, and he asked the company's board to withdraw its offer. The battle went public as Hewlett launched a Web site, www.votenohpcompaq.com, and took out newspaper ads opposing the deal.

HP fired back with its own Web site and newspaper ads, sometimes accusing Hewlett of lying. The company argued that its founders would have supported the purchase. By the end of February 2002, HP said it had enough votes to secure the deal. The deal was finally approved, and by May Fiorina was announcing leadership changes and new product strategy. With the merger, the new HP almost matches industry leader IBM in size and revenue. The new HP claims about 20 percent of the worldwide PC market and remains committed to introducing new products.

David Packard

Born: September 7, 1912
Pueblo, Colorado
Died: March 26, 1996
Palo Alto, California
Cofounder, Hewlett-Packard Company

David Packard.
Reproduced courtesy of the
Library of Congress.

"We wanted to direct our efforts toward making important technical contributions to the advancement of science, industry, and human welfare.... Right from the beginning, Bill and I knew we didn't want to be a 'me too' company merely copying products already on the market."

When he formed Hewlett-Packard (HP) with his partner William "Bill" Hewlett (1913–2001), David Packard honored his personal pledge to advance science and technology. HP introduced several innovative products, including the handheld calculator and the ink-jet printer. It also influenced other businesses with its management style. Packard insisted that managers stay in contact with employees, and he practiced what he called "management by walking around." HP workers called him Dave, and they recounted stories that showed he was just one of the gang, not the wealthy owner of a leading technology company.

Friends in Science

Pueblo, Colorado, still had the feel of the old Wild West when David Packard was born there on September 7, 1912. His father was a lawyer and his mother was a high school teacher. The family lived on a prairie not far from the Rocky Mountains, and Packard had a lifelong love of the outdoors. (After his success at HP, Packard bought ranches in California and Idaho.)

Packard was fascinated by electronics at an early age. He built his first radio in elementary school and joined the radio club at Centennial High School. He also excelled in sports, playing football, basketball and track. In 1930, Packard enrolled at Stanford University to study electrical engineering. During his first semester, he met William Hewlett, another freshman at the school. They often took the same classes, but their friendship didn't develop until their senior year.

David Packard built his first radio using a vacuum tube—a common device in early electronic equipment—two batteries, and a few other parts. With this simple radio, he picked up a station 600 miles away.

The two men were different in some ways: Hewlett was short and stocky, Packard was tall and lean. Hewlett came from a wealthy family, while Packard worked in a local cafeteria to earn extra money. But they shared a love of the outdoors and electronics. In 1934, they talked about starting a business with several other classmates. That plan, however, was delayed when Packard took a job at General Electric (GE) in Schenectady, New York.

Packard spent four years at GE, learning more about electronics and picking up management skills. He and Hewlett stayed in contact, and had their first official business meeting in August 1937 with plans to start a firm called the Engineering Service Company. Packard took a leave of absence from GE the next year, shortly after marrying Lucile Salter. Returning to Palo Alto, he began his partnership with Hewlett while taking classes and working nights.

Creating the HP Way

By the end of 1938, Packard and Hewlett had their first product ready for sale. They discovered that each partner had his own talents. As Packard wrote in *The HP Way,* "Bill was better trained in circuit technology and I was better trained and more experienced in manufacturing processes. This combination of abilities was particularly useful in designing and manufacturing electronics products."

World War II (1939–45) fueled the company's growth. With Hewlett serving in the army, Packard ran the company.

Carleton Fiorina: Breaking the Glass Ceiling

For decades, female executives have struggled to reach the top spots at major U.S. corporations. Some people claimed a "glass ceiling," put in place by corporate boards, let women see the opportunities available, but kept them from reaching those positions. In July 1999, Hewlett-Packard helped crack the glass ceiling when it named Carleton "Carly" Fiorina its president and chief executive officer (CEO). She became the first female to lead a major high-tech business, and the CEO of the largest U.S. company ever run by a woman. In 2000, HP also made her chairwoman of the board.

Fiorina was born in California in 1954. Like HP founders William Hewlett and David Packard, she graduated from Stanford University, although her specialty was medieval history, not electronics. She con-

Carleton Fiorina.
Reproduced by permission of Corbis Corporation (Bellevue).

The HP plant operated all day long, and Packard often slept there on a cot. His wife also worked for the company, serving as a secretary and bookkeeper. Later, Lucile Packard bought presents for HP workers who got married or had a baby. Packard credited his wife with starting many of the traditions that helped make HP feel like a family.

After the war, HP recruited new scientists and managers, and the business grew quickly. As the company expanded, Packard was not able to have direct contact with all the employees, as he once had. He and Hewlett decided to hold a two-day meeting with senior managers to make sure they knew how to treat customers and employees, and to let the managers help shape the company's goals.

sidered a career in law (her father was a judge), then worked at a number of jobs before earning a master's of business administration (MBA) from the University of Maryland. In 1980, she began working in sales for AT&T, then moved up the corporate ladder and earned a second master's degree in 1988.

When AT&T formed **Lucent Technologies** (see entry) to make and sell telephone and Internet equipment, Fiorina took a top position at the new company. In 1998, she was named president of Lucent's largest group, and *Fortune* named her the most powerful woman in business. She won the honor a second time shortly after taking the job at HP.

Fiorina's appointment won her and HP prominent attention in the press. She, however, insisted on downplaying her historical role as the most powerful U.S. businesswoman ever. Instead she focused on the job of adding spark to an old business while continuing the HP tradition. Fiorina faced resistance from some HP employees, as she came across as flashy and tough. Slowly, however, she won support from top managers and the board of directors. By 2001, however, Fiorina was still struggling to change HP.

The battle to take control of Compaq raised questions in the media about Fiorina's commitment to the legendary HP Way. She told the *San Jose Mercury News* that the first objective of the HP Way was to make a profit, and that was what she was after. "If you don't make money," she said, "then all this other stuff isn't possible—you can't preserve jobs, you can't innovate, you can't contribute to the community."

From HP to D.C.

HP always encouraged its employees to be active in the community and give time to others. Packard's outside service included serving as chairman of the board of trustees for Stanford University during the late 1950s. In that position, he met Congressman Mel Laird. In December 1968, Laird was named U.S. secretary of defense by President-elect Richard Nixon (1913–1994). Laird then asked Packard to come to Washington to serve as his deputy secretary.

Some people outside of government questioned Packard's appointment. He had almost no political experience, and HP had contracts with the military worth $100 million, raising the possibility of a conflict of interest. Packard, however, was easily confirmed for the job. While in Washington, he used the HP Way, meeting with military leaders and getting their input on budget cuts. He also set up new methods for purchasing military equipment.

Packard served as the United States was fighting the Vietnam War (1959–75), a conflict that divided many Americans. Working for the Defense Department was difficult during those years, and Packard was often criticized by politicians and the media. He also found it hard to work with the government bureaucracy—the layers of officials who decide what gets done and how. Packard wrote in *The HP Way* that dealing with the bureaucracy was "like pushing on one end of a forty-foot rope, and trying to get the other end to do what you want!" Packard left his position at the end of 1971, although he later served on several government commissions that addressed defense issues.

Last Days at HP

Packard returned to Hewlett-Packard in 1972 and resumed his role as chairman of the board. During the next several years, he made two trips to China. On the second, Packard began a relationship with Chinese officials that led to a joint venture in 1985. During this period, both Packard and Hewlett were not involved in HP's daily operations. Their roles changed, however, in 1990, when HP faced a slowdown. Packard especially took a more active role in the company, helping to reorganize the computer operations. He finally stepped down as chairman of the board in 1993.

Throughout his career, Packard was extremely generous, giving money to Stanford, the Monterey Bay (California) Aquarium, and the David and Lucile Packard Foundation. In 1988, he gave the foundation Hewlett-Packard shares worth $2 billion. After Packard died in 1996, the foundation received the rest of his fortune. Some of the money was used by the foundation's Children, Families, and Communities Program to help minority children. Packard used his scientific and business achievements to advance human welfare, just as he had hoped.

For More Information

Books
Packard, David. *The HP Way*. New York: HarperBusiness, 1995.

Periodicals

Allen, Frederick E. "Present at the Creation." *American Heritage* (May-June 2001): p. 21.

"Carly Fiorina: Catching the Big Mo." *Business Week* (February 18, 2002): p. 46.

"Compaq: Fiorina's Folly or HP's Only Way Out?" *Time* (September 17, 2001): p. 46.

Hardy, Quentin. "The Cult of Carly." *Forbes* (December 13, 1999): p. 138.

"Hewlett Explains Why He Opposes HP-Compaq Deal." *San Jose Mercury News* (February 1, 2002).

"Hewlett-Packard Chief Executive Discusses Battle for Merger." *San Jose Mercury News* (February 22, 2002).

King, Peter H. "One Who Took the High Road." *Los Angeles Times* (March 31, 1996): p. 1.

Lohr, Steve. "It's the Scion vs. the Board in Merger Fight." *New York Times* (February 4, 2002): p. C4.

Nee, Eric. "Open Season on Carly." *Fortune* (July 23, 2001): p. 114.

Saporito, Bill. "Hewlett-Packard Discovers Marketing." *Fortune* (October 1, 1984): p. 50.

"$2 Billion Poorer." *The Economist* (May 7, 1988): p. 26.

Weigner, Kathleen K. "Back into the Race." *Forbes* (October 10, 1983): p.30.

———. "Good-bye to the HP Way?" *Forbes* (November 26, 1990): p. 36.

Zesiger, Sue. "Cover Girl Storms Silicon Valley." *Fortune* (August 16, 1999): p. 29.

Web Sites

Agilent Technologies. [On-line] http:// www.agilent.com.org (accessed on August 15, 2002).

Hewlett-Packard Company. [On-line] http://www.hp.com (accessed on August 15, 2002).

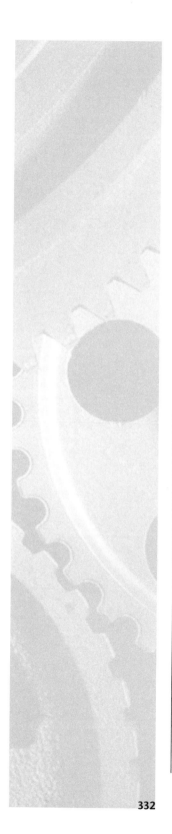

Home Depot, Inc.

2455 Paces Ferry Road
Atlanta, GA 30339-4024
(770) 433-8211
www.homedepot.com

The subtitle of their 1999 book, *Built From Scratch,* tells their story in a nutshell: "How a Couple of Regular Guys Grew the Home Depot from Nothing to $30 billion." In this case, the "regular guys" are Bernie Marcus and Arthur Blank, longtime friends and founders of Home Depot, Inc. Since they started the company more than twenty years ago, the two men have weathered downturns in the economy, lawsuits, competition, and other adversities to become the world's largest chain of home improvement stores. Today, Home Depot has fourteen hundred stores, more than a quarter of a million employees, and sales of nearly $60 billion per year.

Thank Ming the Merciless

The Home Depot story started in the early 1970s when Marcus and Blank were executives at Handy Dan, a chain of home improvement stores owned by the now-defunct Daylin Corporation. The owner of Daylin, Sandy Sigoloff, called himself Ming the Merciless, after a villain from the Flash Gordon movie serials of the 1930s. His management style was ruthless, reflecting his nickname, and he was proud of it. In 1978, Sigoloff fired Marcus and Blank. As it turned out, being fired was one of the best things that ever happened to them.

Losing their jobs allowed the two friends to develop an idea Marcus had been thinking about for several years—opening a chain of hardware and home improvement superstores across the country unlike anything that existed at the time. Marcus and Blank drew on the experiences of two other friends and retailers: **Sam Walton**, founder of **Wal-Mart** (see entry), and Sol Price, founder of the Price Club. The pair also sought financial help from another friend who had been fired by Sigoloff, Texas billionaire H. Ross Perot (1930–).

Home Depot at a Glance

- **Employees:** 251,488
- **CEO:** Robert L. Nardelli
- **Subsidiaries:** EXPO Design Center; Maintenance Warehouse; Georgia Lighting; Apex Supply Company; Your "other" Warehouse; Home Depot Commercial Direct Division; Total HOME
- **Notable Stores:** Home Depot; EXPO Design Center; Villager's Hardware; Del Norte
- **Major Competitors:** Lowe's; Menard; TruServ

When their deal with Perot fell through, Marcus and Blank got the $2 million they needed from another group of investors; they were given two years to get their business started. With money in hand, the pair was ready to go. They leased three vacant buildings from J.C. Penney in Atlanta, Georgia, deciding that city was the best place to launch their first stores. They secured another loan of $3.5 million, which they used to purchase inventory. They also hired twenty employees to help run the management end of the business. On June 22, 1979, the first three Home Depot stores, staffed by two hundred workers, opened in Atlanta. The company began with Marcus as chairman of the board of directors and chief executive office (CEO), and Blank as president.

Constantly Building

Although Home Depot had $7 million in sales its first year, it lost $2 million. In 1980, it opened a fourth store in Atlanta and added one hundred employees, which helped boost sales to $22 million that year. From there, the company grew

Timeline

1979: Bernie Marcus and Arthur Blank open the first three Home Depot stores in Atlanta, Georgia.

1981: Home Depot offers its stock to the public; opens stores in Florida.

1983: Stores open in Arizona and Louisiana.

1985: Company posts sales of $700 million; opens stores in California.

1988: Home Depot has ninety-six stores at year's end.

1990: Annual sales reach $3.8 billion at 145 stores.

1991: Company opens first EXPO Design Center in San Diego, California.

1993: Home Depot expands into Pacific Northwest.

1994: Company opens stores in Canada; annual sales are $12.5 billion.

1997: Blank replaces Marcus as CEO.

1999: *Built From Scratch* by Marcus and Blank is published.

2001: Company acquires Total HOME, a four-store chain in Mexico; annual sales top $53 billion.

2002: Robert L. Nardelli becomes CEO.

rapidly, opening new stores, and posting increased sales and profits each year. By the end of 1981, Home Depot had eight stores, including its first in Florida. Marcus and Blank took the company's stock public, meaning shares of the company could be purchased by the public on the New York Stock Exchange. This raised just over $4 million. The following year, the stock split three times and the company started an employee stock-purchase plan. This allowed workers to have a percentage of their salary deducted from their paychecks and used to purchase Home Depot stock. In effect, the employees who bought the stock owned part of the company. As of 2002, employees owned about 25 percent of Home Depot stock. The year ended with the company operating ten stores with over one thousand employees. It posted sales of $118 million.

From 1982 to 1983, the company doubled in size. With openings in Arizona and Louisiana, Home Depot ended 1983 with nineteen stores, over two thousand employees, and $250 million in sales. One of the reasons for the huge success of the company was its shrewd strategy of purchasing large quantities of an item at a very low price and then reselling the item at only a slight profit. These "advertised specials" worked to bring large numbers of people into the stores to buy a specific product. While in the store, many customers then purchased other merchandise.

For example, in 1981 Blank found a supply of ceiling fans that he was able to get for $27 each. Although these fans would normally be marked up to retail for about $50, Blank priced them at $30. This means the company would make only a $2.00 profit per fan. Such a low profit margin was relatively unheard of in hardware and home improvement stores at the time. But what the company may have lost in a low markup, it made up for in volume. Three days after the sale was advertised, the stores had sold forty thousand fans.

Company Values

From the start, Blank and Marcus felt that offering exceptional customer service was one of the keys to success. "If I ever saw an associate [salesperson] point a customer towards what they needed three aisles over, I would threaten to bite their finger," Marcus wrote in *Built From Scratch*. "I would say, 'Don't ever let me see you point. You take the customer by the hand, and you bring them right where they need to be and you help them.'"

Marcus and Blank also established a set of core values for the Home Depot, which they believe should apply to any company. These included:

- Doing whatever it takes to build customer loyalty.

- Treating all employees with respect, including always paying more than the minimum wage.

- Developing an entrepreneurial spirit that allows many decisions to be made at the store level. Marcus and Blank thought of the Home Depot's organizational structure as an inverted pyramid, with stores and customers at the top and senior management on the bottom.

- Showing respect to all people, regardless of race, religion, gender, income, or education.

- Giving back to the community, not just by donating money to charitable causes, but by encouraging employees to actively take part in such efforts by donating their time and experience.

Marcus said other companies could easily copy this system, but that it would not work unless company management truly believed in the ideal underlying the values. He wrote in *Built From Scratch*, "These values are our company. They are our belief system and we believe in them as much today as we did

H. Ross Perot (1930–) did not help Bernie Marcus and Arthur Blank launch Home Depot because of a quirky situation over the type of automobile Marcus drove. When Perot found out Marcus drove a Cadillac, the billionaire told him that all his executives had to drive Chevrolets. In their book, *Built From Scratch*, Marcus wrote of Perot, "If this guy is going to be bothered by what kind of car I'm driving, how much aggravation are we going to have when we have to make really big decisions?"

when the first Home Depot stores opened in June 1979. Without them, we're no different than our competition.

Do-It-Yourself Philosophy

From 1984 through 1989, the company continued to steadily expand. By the end of 1989, Home Depot had 118 stores from coast to coast, 17,500 employees, and annual sales of $2.7 billion. During 1987, sales increased by 45 percent. This came not only from opening new stores, but also from increasing sales at existing stores by 18 percent. For most retail chains at the time, a 5 percent increase was considered good.

Much of this success is because Home Depot convinced people that they could do many home repairs and improvements themselves. According to a 1988 article in *Fortune*, "What sets Home Depot apart from mere discounters is the company's mission to make a Mr. or Ms. Fixit out of someone who thinks

Putting Values to the Test

In 2001, Bernie Marcus and Arthur Blank showed that they truly believed in leading by example when they both agreed not to accept bonuses they were entitled to. The combined amount was $5 million. At the time, the company was going through budget cuts because of declining profits. Just a few years earlier, however, Home Depot had a chink taken out of its corporate values armor. In 1997, the company settled four gender discrimination lawsuits, although it did not admit having done anything wrong. Home Depot agreed to pay a total of $104 million. Of this, the company paid $65 million to thousands of female workers on the West Coast, $22.5 million in legal fees, and $17 million to overhaul its employment programs. As part of the agreement, Home Depot also set up a procedure to help more women get sales and management jobs within the company.

about calling the plumber to change the bath water." From almost the beginning, the stores offered a wide variety of free classes, ranging from how to replace a toilet to building a patio deck. This became particularly important whenever there was a slump in new home construction because of a poor economy. Instead of buying a new house, many people took on remodeling projects and they turned to Home Depot for help and supplies.

The 1990s saw a ten-fold increase in annual company sales, going from $3.8 billion in 1990 to $38.4 billion in 1999. By the end of the decade, Home Depot had 930 stores and 201,000 employees. It also established two specialty stores: EXPO Design Center and Villager's Hardware. The first EXPO Design Center opened in San Diego, California, in 1991. The stores are 150,000 square-feet, and feature eight interior design departments, including kitchen, bath, lighting, and carpeting. As of 2002, Home Depot had forty-eight EXPOs in fourteen states. The first Villager's Hardware, the company's attempt to get into the $50 billion a year convenience hardware market, opened in 1999 in East Brunswick, New Jersey. But after only three years and four stores, Home Depot scrapped the idea and converted the stores into Home Depots in 2002.

In 2000, the company acquired Apex Supply Company, a wholesale distributor of plumbing, followed by the purchase of Your "other" Warehouse, a specialty plumbing-supply store chain, in 2001. With an eye to the international market, Home Depot bought Total HOME, a four-store chain in Mexico, in 2001. In 2002, it purchased Del Norte, a four-store chain in Juarez, Mexico. It planned to open two more Del Nortes in Mexico by the end of the year.

The sales associates at Home Depot stores are often able to teach customers how to use the tools and products they are buying.
Reproduced by permission of Getty Images.

As of June 2002, Home Depot had a total of 1,400 stores, including 83 in Canada, seven in Puerto Rico, and four in Mexico, and 251,488 employees. It posted $53.6 billion in sales in 2001. The company leadership underwent a dramatic change in January 2002 when cofounder Blank resigned as CEO (he had taken over the position in 1997). He was replaced by president Robert L. Nardelli. Marcus left the board of directors in May 2002, when he reached the company's mandatory retirement age of seventy-two.

Growth Scaled Back

With Nardelli at the helm, Home Depot has scaled back on it growth plans for the immediate future. Marcus had projected that the company would add about three hundred to four hundred new stores a year; Nardelli cut that projected number to about two hundred a year through 2004. He does, however,

Home Depot's tall aisles help keep them well-stocked with in-demand items.

Reproduced by permission of Getty Images.

plan to expand into the service arena, adding such things as carpet installation, lawn care, and pest control.

In light of all the changes, Nardelli intends to address complaints that Home Depot has lost some of its commitment to customer service, including Marcus's original vow that when a customer asks where a product is, the employee will take the customer to where it is. "We've got to make our stores more shoppable, more navigable," Nardelli said in a 2002 *Money* interview. "While we're No. 1 in home improvement, I want to make sure we're No. 1 in every segment of home improvement."

Bernie Marcus

Born: 1930
Newark, New Jersey
Cofounder, Home Depot, Inc.

Bernie Marcus has indeed been successful, building the world's largest chain of home improvement stores in just under twenty-five years, aided by Arthur Blank, his friend and partner. And while the path to success did have obstacles, Marcus viewed the challenges as learning experiences that helped him become a better businessman and person.

Strong Family Foundation

Marcus, the child of Jewish immigrants from Russia, grew up in a low-income neighborhood of Newark, New Jersey, with two older brothers and a sister. His father was a cabinet maker and his mother a homemaker. The family was poor and his father worked fifteen hours a day, seven days a week just to make ends meet. When his brothers were old enough to work, they got jobs to help support the family. When he was eleven years old, Marcus joined a neighborhood gang and soon rose to become its second in command. Realizing that this was not the kind of atmosphere they wanted their children to grow up in, his parents moved to a better neighborhood

"Why have I been successful my whole life? Because I've always surrounded myself with people who are better than I am. That's one of the lessons that guided Arthur Blank and me when we started the Home Depot, and one that every businessperson in America needs to learn."

341

By the time he was seventeen years old, Bernie Marcus had developed an interest in the medical field and decided he wanted to become a psychiatrist. He became interested in the science of the mind after he learned how to hypnotize people.

when he was twelve, despite the additional financial burden this posed.

Marcus has always credited his parents for his success, and acknowledged that they instilled in him a strong religious faith and a positive attitude. He recalled his mother frequently using the Jewish word *b'sheirt,* meaning "it is destined to be." According to Marcus, she would find good in any situation and always focused on the future. In *Built From Scratch,* Marcus wrote, "My mom taught me most of the beliefs I possess today, especially … that the way you handle and deal with life's setbacks creates the basis for what you'll accomplish in the future."

Marcus started working when he was thirteen, getting a job as a soda jerk at an ice cream soda fountain. A soda jerk is someone who scoops ice cream and waits on customers. He also worked as a busboy during summer vacations while in high school. After graduating from high school, Marcus enrolled in the pre-med program at Rutgers College in Newark. During his second year, he applied for a scholarship to Harvard Medical School in Cambridge, Massachusetts. There was some trouble surrounding the scholarship, and he ended up not accepting it.

Turns to Business

Disillusioned, Marcus quit college and went to Florida where he lived for a year. But his mother convinced him to return to Rutgers, where he enrolled in pharmacy school. He graduated in 1954, and became partners in a pharmacy where he worked for nearly a year. His heart was not in the job, however, and he quit to work at a retail cosmetics store in New York City. But the company was not making a profit and Marcus left to take a job with Two Guys, a discount department store chain. By 1959, he was in charge of about $1 billion worth of business.

In 1968, Marcus moved to California where he went to work for a manufacturing company. In 1970, he joined the Daylin Corporation, where he was an executive with its Handy Dan home improvement subsidiary until he was fired in 1978.

The next year, he founded the Home Depot with Arthur Blank, whom he had met while at Handy Dan. Marcus retired from Home Depot in 2002, having served as CEO and chairman of the board of directors. He and his wife, Billi, have a son, Michael Morris. He has a son and daughter, Fred and Suzanne, from a previous marriage.

Life after the Depot

Marcus is the chairman of the Center for Disease Control Foundation and is on the board of directors of a number of organizations, including the New York Stock Exchange. He is active in several community organizations, including the Shepherd Spinal Center and the City of Hope cancer research center. He and his wife are founders of the Marcus Foundation and the Marcus Developmental Resource Center, a support services resource for children with mental impairments and their parents. Marcus has always given generously to many causes, including a $45 million donation in 1998 to help children with brain disorders.

Arthur Blank.
Reproduced by permission of AP/Wide World Photos.

Arthur Blank

Born: 1942
Queens, New York
Cofounder, Home Depot, Inc.

"People often describe me as complex or complicated, and I am probably not an easy man to live with, at home or at work. Part of that comes from my fiercely competitive nature; part of it is my grinding need to climb, to achieve, to do."

Unlike his partner, Bernie Marcus, Arthur Blank does not seem to enjoy being in the limelight. A great majority of the book *Built From Scratch,* which the pair wrote in 1999, is from the perspective of Marcus. While Marcus talks a lot about his childhood, Blank says very little, instead picking up when he entered college. The close relationship, however, between Blank and his father Max is quite evident. He credits his father with teaching him the importance of customer service and the human element in business dealings. "I have such fond memories of my father," Blank wrote. "As a pharmacist, he was always helping people."

Athlete and Scholar

Arthur M. Blank was born in Queens, New York, in 1942. His father worked as a pharmacist and his mother was a housewife. When his father died at age forty-four (Blank was fifteen), his mother was forced to take over the family pharmacy even though she had no previous business experience. In addition, she had Arthur and his brother, Michael, to finish raising.

Academically, Blank was an average student in elementary and high school. He was always athletically inclined, playing baseball and football, and running track in high school. In baseball, he started as a centerfielder but was forced to switch to catcher when he injured his throwing arm. He apparently got his athletic abilities from his father, who excelled in track at Columbia University in New York.

After graduating from high school, Blank attended Babson College, a small business school near Boston, Massachusetts. It was there that he began to take his education seriously. Blank's outgoing personality made him popular with the other students. He was elected vice president of his junior class and president of his senior class. He was a straight-A student and made the dean's list.

With a limited family income, Blank had to help pay his way through college. Since he loved being outdoors, he started his own landscaping business. He also earned money by doing laundry several nights a week for other students. While Blank studied business, his brother majored in pharmaceutical science. The plan was for the two to take over running the family pharmacy from their mother, Molly.

Foregoes Family Business

Blank graduated from Babson in 1963 with a degree in accounting, but he had second thoughts about joining the family pharmacy. Instead, he took a job with the New York accounting firm of Arthur Young & Company where he worked for about five years. In 1968, Blank decided to go to work for the family pharmacy, but he was there for only a few months before his mother sold it to the Daylin Corporation. In 1970, Blank became chief financial officer (CFO) for Elliot's Drug Stores/Stripe Discount Stores, a Daylin subsidiary. Two years later, he became president of the division and moved to Griffin, Georgia, with his wife, Diana, and their three children, Kenny, Dena, and Danielle.

Life after the Depot

In 1974, Daylin sold the Elliot's/Stripe division and Blank went to work for Bernie Marcus at Daylin's Handy Dan

Many people assumed that because Blank cofounded the world's largest home improvement chain, he must be a whiz of a handyman. But Blank was more comfortable with a baseball bat in his hand rather than a hammer. "I never had the opportunity to be handy because I was raised in an apartment," Blank said in *Built From Scratch*. "I was always out in the street, playing ball and running around with my friends. There was nothing made of wood around our house—everything was cement, bricks, and block. I didn't live in a single-family home until I was 31 years old."

division of home improvement stores. He remained there until 1978, when he and Marcus were fired. A year later, the pair started the Home Depot with three stores in Atlanta. He became CEO of the company in 1997, a post he held until he retired in 2000. In 2002, he bought the National Football League's Atlanta Falcons and serves as its president, CEO, and chairman. He lives with his second wife, Stephanie, and their three children, in Atlanta.

Blank is on the board of trustees of the Carter Center, Emory University, the National Conference of Christians and Jews, and the North Carolina Outward Bound School, among others. He is a member of Babson College's Entrepreneurship Advisory Board and Academy of Distinguished Entrepreneurs. He established The Home Depot Entrepreneurial Scholarship program for undergraduates, as well as the Arthur M. Blank Family Foundation. Blank was also recognized by the City of Hope cancer research center for leadership in fund-raising. He and his wife, Stephanie, have donated $73 million to charitable groups.

For More Information

Books

Blank, Arthur M., et al. *Built From Scratch*. New York: Times Books, 1999.

Periodicals

Armour, Lawrence L. "Home Depot: Now It Can Be Told." *Your Company* (May 1, 1999): pp. 18–19.

Blank, Arthur. "They Sweat the Small Stuff." *Canadian Business* (May 28, 1999): pp. 51–55.

Gibbs, Lisa. "Room for Improvement: Home Depot's New CEO Wants to Remodel the Retailer—and Restore a Faded Growth Stock." *Money* (March 1, 2002): p. 33.

Lamm, Marcy. "The Nuts and Bolts of Hardware Success: How Home Depot Captured Imagination." *Atlanta Business Chronicle* (November 6, 1998): p. 3A.

Pellet, Jennifer. "Mr. Fix-It Steps In."*Chief Executive* (October 2001): p. 45.

Saporito, Bill. "The Fix is in at Home Depot."*Fortune* (Feb. 29, 1988): p. 73-76.

"Tidying Up At Home Depot." *Business Week* (November 26, 2001): p. 102.

Web Sites

Home Depot, Inc. [On-line] http://www.homedepot.com (accessed on August 15, 2002).

Kellogg Company

One Kellogg Square, Box 3599
Battle Creek, MI 95014-3599
(616) 961-2000
www.kelloggs.com

The Kellogg Company's South Plant, Battle Creek, Michigan.
Reproduced by permission of AP/Wide World Photos.

For millions of people around the world, breakfast includes a bowl of Kellogg's cereal. Starting with just one product, the Kellogg Company added many other items over the years, targeting sugar-coated cereal at children and offering bran and other healthy grains to adults. In recent years, the company has moved beyond cereal, selling snack bars and other foods that can be eaten on the run.

Since its founding in 1906, the Kellogg Company has relied heavily on advertising to stir demand for its products. The company has also created several well-known cartoon mascots for its leading brands. Generations of children know Tony the Tiger, who roars about Kellogg's "Gr-r-reat" Frosted Flakes, and Toucan Sam, the colorful "spokesbird" for Froot Loops. Even as Kellogg's expands its offerings, cereal remains its most successful product, making the company the world's top cereal producer.

Health Food for Breakfast

The Kellogg Company was born in Battle Creek, Michigan, "the cereal capital of the world." Starting in 1876, Dr. John

Harvey (J. H.) Kellogg ran the Battle Creek Sanitarium, a health spa that promoted a vegetarian diet and forbid its guests from drinking alcohol or smoking cigarettes. Kellogg began experimenting with breakfast foods made from grain, to replace the typical late-nineteenth century breakfast centered around meat, eggs, and other heavy foods. One of Kellogg's first inventions was granola, which combined wheat, oatmeal, and corn meal.

After trying granola at the sanitarium, many guests wanted to eat the cereal at home, so Kellogg established the Sanitas Food Company to make and sell the product. Dr. Kellogg had help running Sanitas from his younger brother Will Keith (W. K.). In 1894, the Kelloggs wanted to make a new wheat product that would be easy to digest. They tried putting boiled wheat through large rollers, hoping to make wheat flakes, but the process was a failure. After one batch of boiled wheat was accidentally left out to dry, the Kelloggs put it through the rollers, and this time the wheat formed small flakes. The brothers then baked the flakes, resulting in the first flaked cereal, which the Kelloggs called Granose.

Kellogg at a Glance

- **Employees:** 28,000
- **CEO:** Carlos M. Gutierrez
- **Subsidiaries:** Argkel; CELNASA; Favorite Food Products; Garden City Bakery Ltd.; Gollek B.V.; K-One Inc.; KFSC, Inc.; Kelarg; Kelcone Ltd.; Kelmill Ltd.; Mountaintop Baking Company; Portable Foods Manufacturing Company Ltd.; Specialty Foods Investment Company; The Eggo Company; Worthington Foods, Inc.
- **Major Competitors:** General Foods; General Mills; Ralston-Purina; Quaker Oats
- **Notable Products:** Corn Flakes; Rice Krispies; Special K; Froot Loops; Frosted Flakes; Pop Tarts; Eggo waffles; Keebler cookies and crackers; Cheez-It crackers; Nutri-Grain bars

Dr. Kellogg served his new cereal at the sanitarium, and Sanitas sold it by mail to former guests. By 1905, the company was also selling corn flakes, producing 150 cases a day. Sanitas had more than forty competitors by then, as other cereal companies sprang up in Battle Creek. W. K. Kellogg wanted to expand the business even more, but his brother disagreed. A biography of the younger Kellogg, *The Original Has This Signature—W. K. Kellogg,* quotes his early thoughts on the business: "If given the opportunity, the food company would develop in such a manner that the sanitarium would be only a side show as to the food business."

 **Timeline**

1906: W. K. Kellogg starts the Battle Creek Toasted Corn Flake Company.

1909: Annual sales of Toasted Corn Flakes reach one million cases.

1914: Kellogg's opens a plant in Canada.

1928: Rice Krispies are introduced.

1938: W. K. Kellogg retires.

1952: Tony the Tiger is first used to promote Frosted Flakes.

1964: Kellogg's introduces Pop Tarts.

1970: Kellogg's buys the Eggo Waffle Company.

1989: Kellogg's sells its first cereal bars.

1999: Carlos M. Gutierrez is named CEO of Kellogg's.

2001: Kellogg's completes its purchase of Keebler Foods.

Kellogg's and Corn Flakes

In 1906, W. K. Kellogg left his brother's sanitarium and founded the Battle Creek Toasted Corn Flake Company, selling a corn flake he had perfected at Sanitas. With his new company, Kellogg had the freedom he wanted to expand the business. He had already shown a genius for marketing, introducing the idea of offering cereal samples door-to-door. With his own company, Kellogg spent one-third of his money on a full-page ad in the *Ladies Home Journal*. Within a year, the Battle Creek Toasted Corn Flake Company sold more than 175,000 cases of its cereal. By 1909, annual sales of Toasted Corn Flakes reached one million cases.

In 1907, Kellogg shortened his company's name to the Toasted Corn Flake Company (later he changed it to the Kellogg Company). The same year, the company's factory was destroyed by fire, but Kellogg quickly built a bigger and better plant. In 1910, Kellogg's gave consumers their first premium—a free gift inside the cereal box—called "The Funny Jungleland Moving Pictures Book." Two years later, the company introduced its second product, Krumbles, a shredded wheat cereal. Over the next several years, Kellogg's brought out two news cereals, 40% Bran Flakes and All-Bran.

Except for a brief time after World War I (1914–18), the Kellogg Company continued to grow. By 1920, the company produced thirty thousand cases of cereal per day in Battle Creek. A Canadian factory had opened in 1914, and the company expanded overseas in 1923, opening a plant in Sydney, Australia.

Guests at the Battle Creek Sanitarium included such business leaders as Harvey Firestone (1868–1938) and **Henry Ford** (see **Ford Motor Company** entry) and the explorer Richard Byrd (1888–1957). Another guest, C. W. Post (1854–1914), ate Kellogg's cereal and then launched his own successful cereal company.

Depression Years and Beyond

In 1929, stock prices crashed, leading to the Great Depression. At a time when many businesses cut advertising costs, Kellogg doubled its budget for ads and profits rose. Kellogg's began sponsoring radio shows for children and introduced cartoon elves called Snap, Crackle, and Pop to sell Rice Krispies, which hit the market in 1928. By the end of the decade, the company had ensured its place as the world's largest cereal company, selling 40 percent of all cereal purchased in the United States and holding more than half of the international market.

By 1939, W. K. Kellogg had stepped down as head of his company, and Chicago banker Watson H. Vanderploeg became president. Kellogg had once hoped to turn control of Kellogg's to his son, John L., who had worked at the company during its early years. In 1925, however, a personal dispute between the two men led to John L. Kellogg's departure from the company. Kellogg then groomed his grandson, John Jr., as the next company head, but that plan did not work either. After a series of health problems, the younger Kellogg committed suicide in 1938. Vanderploeg, however, proved a fine successor, adding new products and taking them into new markets.

In the 1950s, Kellogg's introduced its first sweetened cereals aimed at children. These products included Sugar Smacks and Sugar Frosted Flakes. To sell these new products, the company advertised heavily on television and introduced cartoon characters identified with each brand. The first, Tony the Tiger, appeared in 1952. The company also focused on the diet concerns of adults, launching Special K as a healthy, low-calorie cereal. Later in the decade, Kellogg's introduced a new slogan: "The Best to You Each Morning."

Moving beyond Cereal

In 1964, Kellogg's introduced a new breakfast product, Pop Tarts. Heated in a toaster, these fruit pastries provided a sweet alternative to cold cereal. The company also began adding new products by purchasing other companies. In 1969, it bought Salada Foods, best known for its tea; the next year Kellogg's bought Eggo Waffles, another breakfast food designed for the toaster. Kellogg's also took over Fearn International, a company that sold soups and other foods to restaurants, and several small foreign food companies.

One of the first Kellogg Cornflakes boxes, from 1906.
Reproduced by permission of Archive Photos, Inc.

Some of this expansion came as Kellogg's faced problems with its core cereal business. In 1972, the Federal Trade Commission (FTC) accused Kellogg's and its two major competitors, General Mills and General Foods, of keeping smaller companies out of the cereal market and of overcharging customers. The companies denied the charges and were not penalized. Cereal companies also faced criticism from dentists and other groups who blasted the high sugar content of cereals designed for children. In 1978, sales of Kellogg's sugar-coated cereals fell for the first time. Overall cereal sales were also slowing, as the number of young people in the United States decreased. This segment of the population was traditionally Kellogg's best market. In addition, the company faced competition from store-brand cereals, which cost less than name brands such as Kellogg's.

During the early 1980s, Kellogg's tried to fight slumping sales in several ways. It returned to its Depression-era tactic of spending more on advertising. It also introduced new products. Some were targeted at children. Others, meant for adults, stressed good nutrition. In 1985, company chairman William LaMothe told Forbes, "[Health] is our thing.... Where else can you get such nutrition for twenty cents a serving?" By 1988, Kellogg's increased its annual sales more than 50 percent, going from $2.4 billion (in 1983) to $3.8 billion.

The company also had success with a new type of product, cereal and snack bars. It launched Smart Start Cereal Bars in 1989, then changed the name to Nutri-Grain in 1991. Other bars followed, and Kellogg's eventually became the leading seller of cereal and snack bars. These products were a response to changing eating habits. Fewer Americans were eating breakfast sitting at a table; they wanted food they could eat on their way to school or work. Snack bars promised quick energy boosts or a tasty treat any time during the day.

Problems with Modern Food Technology?

To J. H. and W. K. Kellogg, their cereals were health food. Starting in the 1930s, Kellogg's was the first company to put nutritional information on its packages. Later, during the 1980s, it introduced a number of cereals made from whole grains. While grains are healthier than grain that is heavily processed before it is cooked.

In recent years, however, Kellogg's and other large food companies have been questioned about using genetically modified foods. Scientists can change a crop's genes, the basic chemicals that control how all plants and animals develop and function. Genetically modified plants might grow faster, taste better, or resist insects. Some environmental groups believe these modified foods may be dangerous to humans. The organization Greenpeace has criticized Kellogg's for using genetically modified corn and soybeans in some of its products. In 2001, Kellogg's recalled corn dogs sold under its Morningstar Farms brand, after tests showed it contained traces of modified corn not approved for use in foods.

Surviving in a Constantly Changing Industry

During the early 1900s, Kellogg's sold some of the food companies it had bought earlier to focus on cereal and other breakfast foods. Competition was again tough, as consumers bought even more store-brand products, and major rival General Mills lowered its prices, forcing Kellogg's to follow suit. Overseas, a new partnership between General Mills and Nestle was stealing some of Kellogg's customers.

Once again, Kellogg's fought back with more advertising and new products. In 1997, it opened the W. K. Kellogg Institute for Food and Nutrition Research, where food experts tried to create new items. In 1999, a Kellogg's researcher told *Fortune* the company wanted "to make foods that are tastier, healthier, and easier." The Kellogg Institute's efforts included Rice Krispies Treats, snack bars based on the popular cereal, and an improved Raisin Bran that did not get soggy in milk.

Despite its innovations, Kellogg's saw its cereal sales remain basically flat after 1994. In 2001, the company tried to bolster sales by announcing a deal with the **Walt Disney Company** (see entry). Kellogg's began selling cereal featuring several popular Disney characters on the boxes, including Winnie the Pooh and Mickey Mouse. Kellogg's also took a major step into a new market when it bought Keebler, the second-largest cookie-and-cracker manufacturer in the United States.

After adding Keebler's products, Kellogg's made 60 percent of its sales from cereal, compared to 75 percent before the deal. The year before the Keebler purchase, Kellogg ventured into another new area, buying Worthington Foods, the manufacturer of vegetarian "meat" products. A company founded on corn flakes has moved far beyond breakfast, while remaining a major international food corporation.

W. K. Kellogg

Born: April 7, 1860
Battle Creek, Michigan
Died: October 6, 1951
Battle Creek, Michigan
Founder, Kellogg Company

"Mr. Kellogg appreciated the power of the new force that was beginning to be used by progressive businessmen—
the force of consumer advertising. Visualizing his foods on breakfast tables in millions of homes, he knew that the entrée to these homes was chiefly through advertising."

—*Horace B. Powell, biographer of W. K. Kellogg*

W. K. Kellogg helped discover the process that gave the world flaked cereal, leading to a revolution in breakfast foods. His true genius, however, may have been as a marketer, not an inventor. By the time Kellogg launched his own company to sell toasted corn flakes, more than forty other companies were producing cold cereals. What helped set Kellogg's flakes apart was advertising, as Kellogg used every method possible to sell his "original" corn flake.

Battle Creek Success Story

Willie Keith Kellogg was born in Battle Creek, Michigan, on April 7, 1860, the seventh son of Ann Janette and John Preston Kellogg. Never liking his name, Kellogg later shortened "Willie" to Will. In business, however, he was usually known as W. K. His large family lived simply in Battle Creek, as his father struggled to build a broom-manufacturing business. By the time W. K. was thirteen, he was traveling to local grocery stores selling his father's brooms. Kellogg dropped out of school and worked in the broom business until 1880, when he joined his older brother, Dr. J. H. Kellogg, at the Battle Creek Sanitarium.

At his brother's health resort, Kellogg performed an assortment of roles, from accountant to repairman. His salary was low, despite the long hours he worked and the success of the sanitarium. A diary entry of Kellogg's from 1884 is quoted in his biography, *The Original Has This Signature—W. K. Kellogg*: "I feel kind of blue. Am afraid that I will always be a poor man the way things look now." Little wonder that the younger Kellogg was discouraged since he had to support both his wife Ella and his mother on his small salary. Later, he and Ella had four children.

Some of the Kellogg company's early advertising featured a painting of a young farm girl holding corn. She was known as the "Sweetheart of the Corn." Billboards were also an important part of promoting Kellogg's cereal. In 1912, the company displayed what was then the world's largest advertising sign, standing 106 feet wide and 50 feet high.

Kellogg's duties at the sanitarium included running his brother's book subscription service and managing Sanitas Food Company. Sanitas emerged from Dr. Kellogg's efforts to find nutritious food to serve his guests. The doctor built a test kitchen to experiment with new foods. In 1894, the brothers created a new breakfast product, toasted wheat flakes. W. K. Kellogg insisted the flakes be served whole instead of crushed, as his brother suggested.

Kellogg saw that producing cereals and other health foods could become a huge industry. Selling only by mail and using little advertising, Sanitas did well. Kellogg wanted to expand the business by advertising more, so Sanitas could compete with the new cereal companies popping up in Battle Creek. Dr. Kellogg, however, resisted the idea, just one of many instances where the two brothers clashed. Never close to his older brother, in 1906 W. K. Kellogg left the Sanitas Food Company to start his own business.

The Original Corn Flake

Kellogg decided to concentrate on selling corn flakes, and he called his company the Battle Creek Toasted Corn Flake Company. He perfected the flakes by using corn grits instead of whole corn. Later he added malt to improve their taste. Kellogg once admitted that he didn't know much about selling cereal through grocery stores. But, in *The Original Has This Signature—W. K. Kellogg,* Horace B. Powell quotes him as telling a colleague at the business, "I sort of feel it in my bones that we are preparing a campaign for a food which will eventually prove to be the leading cereal of the United States, if not the world."

Armed with that confidence and a commitment to advertise heavily, Kellogg first sold his flakes under the Sanitas name. On the box was the slogan "The original bears this signature," followed by "W. K. Kellogg" in Kellogg's handwriting. Within a year, Kellogg's name replaced Sanitas on the box, and sales were climbing.

Kellogg's success caught his brother's attention. In 1908, Dr. Kellogg changed the name of his food company to the Kellogg Food Company and began selling corn flakes overseas in packages similar to those his brother used. Business dealing between the two brothers, based on W. K. Kellogg's ties to Sanitas, also strained their relationship. In 1910, Kellogg sued his older brother; the court case dragged on for years. In the end, Kellogg won his suit, although he and Dr. Kellogg rarely spoke again for the rest of their lives.

Cereal Success

Corn flakes and other new products turned Kellogg's into the world's leading cereal manufacturer. Just as he did during his days at the sanitarium, Kellogg worked long hours, often walking through his factories to watch operations. He had a sharp eye for detail and always looked for ways to save money. He demanded hard work from his employees, and some found him distant, even mean. Yet Kellogg paid better-than-average wages for the time and would sometimes help relatives of workers struck by illness or other misfortunes.

By the 1920s, the man who feared he would always be poor was one of the wealthiest business owners in the United States. He owned homes in Michigan and Florida and he raised

A Company Man Takes Control

In 1999, the Kellogg Company chose Carlos M. Gutierrez as its chief executive officer (CEO), and the next year it named him company chairman. Gutierrez, who first started working for Kellogg as a sales representative in Mexico, is one of the few Hispanic Americans to run a major U.S. corporation.

Gutierrez was born in Cuba in 1953. His father owned a pineapple plantation on the island, but the family left Cuba after Fidel Castro (c. 1927–) seized control of the government in 1959. The Gutierrezes fled to Florida and later moved to Mexico. In 1975, Gutierrez was attending the Monterey Institute of Technology when he joined Kellogg. Over the years, he worked his way up through the company, holding important executive positions in Latin America, Canada, and Asia, as well as Battle Creek. In 1990, Gutierrez was named a vice president, and he received several other promotions before taking control of Kellogg's.

One of Gutierrez's first moves as CEO upset some people in Battle Creek, as he closed the old corn flake plant in the city and fired hundreds of workers. He told the Associated Press, "These are painful but necessary decisions to make." At least one business analyst said the company should have made the move years before. Gutierrez then focused on increasing sales by expanding Kellogg's product line. In 2000, while appearing on the business news program *Nightly Business Report*, he said, "We see a great future beyond cereal." Gutierrez added, however, that cereal "will always be very significant to us."

horses on a ranch in California. Although he spent more time away from Battle Creek, he remained active in his company and the community.

In 1930, Kellogg used some of his fortune to start the W. K. Kellogg Foundation. A personal tragedy led to the founding of what remains one of the largest charitable organizations in the United States. Kellogg could not find good medical care for one of his grandsons, who was badly injured in a fall. His foundation, Kellogg said, would help families pay for the care of their injured and sick children. Soon after its founding, the Kellogg Foundation enlarged its focus, contributing to a wide range of charitable causes.

Kellogg retired from the Kellogg Company in 1938, but he remained chairman of the board of directors. The year before, he had been diagnosed with glaucoma, an eye disease. His eyesight worsened, and he was blind for the last ten years of his life. With the help of a seeing-eye dog, he still visited the Battle Creek plant and participated in his foundation's activities. Kellogg died in 1951 at the age of ninety-one. Decades after his death, the signature of his last name still appears on Kellogg's products.

For More Information

Books

Powell, Horace B. *The Original Has This Signature—W. K. Kellogg.* Englewood Cliffs, NJ: Prentice-Hall, 1956.

Periodicals

Jones, Terry Yue. "Outside the Box." *Forbes* (June 14, 1999): p. 52.

"Kellogg's Recalls StarLink-tainted Corn Dogs." United Press International (March 15, 2001).

Murray, Barbara. "Cereal Bars Continue to Fly off the Shelves." *Supermarket News* (May 7, 2001): p. 123.

"One on One with Kellogg's CEO, Carlos Gutierrez." *Nightly Business Report* (February 23, 2000).

Sellers, Patricia. "How King Kellogg's Beat the Blahs." *Fortune* (August 29, 1988): p. 54.

Serwer, Andrew. "What Price Brand Loyalty?" *Fortune* (January 10, 1999): p. 103.

Taylor, Alex, III. "Kellogg's Cranks Up Its Idea Machine." *Fortune* (July 5, 1999): p. 181.

Willoughby, Jack. "The Snap, Crackle, Pop Defense." *Forbes* (March 25, 1985): p. 82.

Web Sites

Kellogg Company. [On-line] http://www.kelloggs.com (accessed on August 15, 2002).

W. K. Kellogg Foundation. [On-line] http://www.wkkf.org (accessed on August 15, 2002).

Kmart Corporation

3100 West Big Beaver Road
Troy, MI 48084
(248) 463-1000
www.kmartcorp.com

K mart began as one of the first discount stores. They were also called "five-and-dimes" because each item in the store could be purchased for five or ten cents. Soon after it opened, because of good management and fair prices, Kmart became the top discount retailer in the United States. It was even more successful than Woolworth, the company that introduced the idea of variety discount stores. Eventually the success of Kmart caused the decline and the closing of Woolworth stores.

The story then repeated itself. Kmart became the leader of discount stores, but because of poor management and overspending, new discount stores on the block, including **Wal-Mart** and **Target** (see entries), began to take over, leaving Kmart with too many stores, too few customers, and not enough money to stay in business. The fate of the historic retailer, however, has yet to be determined. Plans to close unprofitable stores and revitalize older ones are the company's latest efforts to restore Kmart's fading image.

Kmart at a Glance

- **Employees:** 252,000

- **CEO:** James B. Adamson

- **Subsidiaries:** BlueLight.com, LLC

- **Major Competitors:** Wal-Mart Stores, Inc., Target Corporation, Sears

- **Notable Stores:** Kmart stores; Kmart Supercenters

Nickels and Dimes Add Up to Millions

S. S. Kresge understood the value of a dollar. He worked hard for his money and spent it carefully. While working as a bookkeeper in a hardware store in 1889, Kresge noticed that customers who purchased store merchandise on credit, rather than paying cash, bought a lot of items without thinking because they were not handing over their hard-earned dollars right at the time of the sale. Kresge also believed that allowing customers to buy on credit caused the store to lose money because products went out but cash did not come in.

He was impressed by the way the new discount stores did business. Frank W. Woolworth (1852–1919) was the founder of the first "Great 5-Cent Store" and John McCrory (1860–1943) later established McCrory discount stores. At both businesses, customers had to pay cash for their purchases. According to Kresge, this would make customers spend their money more wisely.

Kresge wanted to go into business with Woolworth, but Woolworth turned him down. Instead, he joined McCrory, who had a chain of six "bazaar" stores and two five-and-ten cent stores. In 1897, Kresge gave McCrory $8,000 and became an equal partner in his business. They opened stores in Memphis, Tennessee, and Detroit, Michigan. Two years later, Kresge became sole manager of the Detroit store and eventually paid McCrory $3,000 to end their partnership and give up his share of the Memphis store.

Soon Kresge found another partner, his brother-in-law Charles J. Wilson. He also established his headquarters in Detroit. From 1900 to 1907 the partners opened stores in eight cities: Detroit; Port Huron, Michigan; Toledo, Ohio; Cleveland, Ohio; Columbus, Ohio; Pittsburgh, Pennsylvania; Indianapolis, Indiana; and Chicago, Illinois. By 1912 Kresge bought out Wilson, changed the company's name to S. S. Kresge, and expanded to eighty-five stores with annual sales of $10 million.

 **Timeline**

1899: S. S. Kresge establishes S. S. Kresge Company.

1912: Kresge has eighty-five stores and $10 million in sales.

1962: First Kmart store opens in suburb of Detroit, Michigan.

1966: S. S. Kresge dies; sales top the $1 billion mark.

1977: Kresge name changes to Kmart Corporation.

1984: Kmart acquires Walden Book Company and Builders Square.

1987: Martha Stewart is introduced as Kmart's entertainment and lifestyle spokesperson and consultant.

1990: Company purchases Sports Authority and acquires OfficeMax.

1992: Company acquires Borders.

1997: The new Big Kmart format and logo is launched.

1999: Company introduces BlueLight.com.

2000: Charles Conaway becomes CEO.

2001: The Blue Light Special is reintroduced.

2002: Kmart files for Chapter 11 bankruptcy protection; company undergoes management reorganization.

Second only to Woolworth dime stores, Kresge's had become a household name for cost-conscious shoppers throughout the Midwest and Northeast.

After World War I (1914–18), inflation caused prices everywhere to rise quickly, which made it difficult for dime stores to maintain their low prices. To stay in business, Kresge opened "green front" stores, selling items for twenty-five cents to one dollar, next to the traditional five- and ten-cent "red front" stores. Kresge's and Woolworth's, which also had red and green front stores, were most often located in high-traffic downtown areas. This was before suburban areas were developed in areas surrounding larger cities. By the mid-1930s, Kresge opened

The Five-and-Dime

A customer went to a five-and-dime store to purchase all sorts of items contained under one roof. Adults might find purses, animal soap, shaving brushes, or police whistles. Children could purchase supplies like pencils, tablets of paper, a box of sixteen crayons, white paste, boy's ties, girl's hair ribbons, and pocket combs—all for ten cents or less. Dime stores were also popular for their lunch counters where customers could sit on stools at a counter and enjoy lunch, drinks, and sweets for twenty-five cents or less. In 1899, the typical wage earned by a five-and-dime counter girl was $2.50 to $3.00 per week.

his first store in a suburban shopping center in Kansas City, Missouri, eventually selling items for hundreds of dollars.

The First Kmart

By the 1950s, five-and-dime stores had become known as variety stores because they sold a variety of items at low prices. Kresge's was one of many variety stores, and competition was fierce. In 1959, a thirty-year Kresge employee, Harry B. Cunningham (1907–1992), was promoted to company president. Under his leadership the company made some changes that would eventually make it the number one discount store.

Cunningham researched other discount stores and visited all of the Kresge stores. He determined the company would make more money if it purchased large amounts of a small number of items and discounted their prices. With this innovation, the Kresge company invested $80 million to build a chain of discount stores. The chain was called Kmart, and in 1962, the first store opened in Garden City, Michigan, a suburb of Detroit.

The 1960s and 1970s were times of great expansion. In 1966, the year Sebastian Kresge died, S. S. Kresge Corporation owned 162 Kmart stores, 753 Kresge stores, 100 Jupiter stores (Kresge stores located in deteriorating business areas that were renamed "Jupiter"), and 108 Canadian stores. In 1977, because the Kmart stores provided more than 90 percent of Kresge sales, the company changed its name to the Kmart Corporation.

By the beginning of 1980, Kmart's rapid expansion started taking its toll on the existing stores. They began losing customers to businesses that offered lower prices, were better organized, and sold higher quality merchandise. To stay competitive, Kmart began to upgrade their stores and the quality of their products. The company also implemented a modern

computer system and improved the way it distributed its merchandise.

Spread Too Thin

In another effort to boost the company's income, Kmart Corporation began to expand by purchasing other companies. From 1984 to 1992, Kmart acquired Walden Book Company, Builders Square (a chain of home improvement stores), Payless Drugs Northwest, PACE Membership Warehouse, The Sports Authority, OfficeMax, and Borders bookstores. In addition, they introduced Designer Depot stores, which specialized in off-price apparel, or brand-named merchandise reduced to very low prices. In 1987, the company began one of the most important associations in its history: introducing **Martha Stewart** (see **Martha Stewart Living Omnimedia, Inc.** entry) as Kmart's entertainment and lifestyle spokesperson and consultant.

K mart will always be recognized as the home of the Blue Light Special, an in-store advertising campaign where a flashing blue light, accompanied by the announcement "Attention, Kmart shoppers ...," alerted customers about a spontaneous sale. This technique was copied from the blue plate special in 1940s restaurants.

Even with the help of Martha Stewart and her products, Kmart continually fell behind its competitors. Wal-Mart had become the nation's number one retailer in January 1991. Throughout the 1990s and into 2000, Kmart tried to win back old customers and attract new ones. In 1991, it opened Kmart Supercenters, which carried both groceries and general merchandise and was open twenty-four hours, seven days a week. In 1997, the company introduced a new Big Kmart store format and logo for renovated and updated stores, and in 1999, BlueLight.com was launched, which provided free Internet access.

In order to make enough money to complete all of the renovations, Kmart had to sell the retail chains that it had purchased earlier in the decade like Borders, OfficeMax, and Builders Squares. The company also tried new advertising campaigns, including chatty television commercials featuring popular comedian and talk-show host Rosie O'Donnell (1962–) and director Penny Marshall (1943–).

In the spring of 1998 it looked like Kmart might be revived. The company reported earnings of $47 million, which was triple the amount that had been reported in 1997. According to financial analysts, however, the growth was partially due to the strength of the consumer economy. Kmart still had a long way to go to surpass its competitors and resume its number one position.

Struggling to Survive

After the period of expansion and growth ended, Kmart needed a new plan for survival. In 2000, they recruited Charles Conaway, an executive from drugstore chain CVS, to help with reorganization. "Kmart has been in need of some new blood, and I think this is a step in the right direction," financial analyst Jeffrey Edelman said in a 2000 *New York Times* article.

One of the ways Conaway tried to compete with Wal-Mart was to reintroduce the "Blue Light Special" in 2001, ten years after it was discontinued. This time it was promoted as the "Blue Light Always" campaign, with disco-dancing blue lights and $25 million worth of of ads saying that prices had been cut on thirty-eight thousand items. Prices for almost all items, however, were still lower at Wal-Mart. The campaign failed, and Kmart was in worse shape than ever.

By January 2002, customers were complaining. They claimed that advertised items were not always in stock, Kmart stores were messy, Wal-Mart had better prices, and Target offered more stylish options. The company had lost so much money that Kmart decided to file for Chapter 11 bankruptcy protection. Filing Chapter 11 bankruptcy gives the company time to form a business plan to get back up on its feet. Part of Kmart's plan involved closing its most unprofitable stores, which included over two hundred Kmart discount stores and twelve Kmart Supercenter retail outlets in forty states, and one Kmart store in Puerto Rico.

A few months later, Kmart reported a $2.4 billion loss from the previous year and an additional $1 billion loss for a five-week period ending May 1, 2002. "The challenge is tougher than ever," said Keith Naughton, author of a 2002 *Newsweek* article, "now that Kmart's identity crisis … has morphed into a financial crisis." But troubles only got worse. In May, the FBI announced that it was investigating the company for "possible criminal violations." Many of Kmart's former management team were also being investigated.

 ## The Martha and Kmart Partnership

In 1987, when Martha Stewart joined Kmart as the company's spokesperson, the store was the nation's biggest discount chain with sales of $23.99 billion. Ten years later, Kmart introduced Martha's Everyday Collection. A 1997 *Time* article reported that the collection offered "Kmart's shoppers (median income: $35,000) the kind of items that Martha might buy, at an affordable price." The collection consisted of bed and bath fashions and a 256-color paint line. Later, the collection expanded to include such items as garden tools, patio furniture, live plants and seeds, houseware essentials, storage helpers and organizers, and home decorating products.

The relationship between Stewart and Kmart became strained after the company filed for bankruptcy in 2002. The celebrity and the discount retailer agreed, however, that as long as Kmart was able to pay Stewart's company for the products it sold, Stewart's contract would extend until 2008. To show her support and boost sales, Stewart appeared in a TV commercial directed by Spike Lee (1957–). The "Stuff of Life" ad, which aired in May 2002, promoted Stewart's Everyday product line and urged viewers to go to Kmart.

Discount shoppers navigate the newly renovated aisles of the brighter Super Kmart store.
Reproduced by permission of AP/Wide World Photos.

That same month CEO Charles Conaway was replaced by James B. Adamson, and as of June 2002, the company continued to undergo reorganization. Adamson and other Kmart executives remained hopeful and projected a revival for the company by spring 2004. According to Adamson in *Supermarket News,* "While there is still much hard work ahead, we are pleased with the progress we are making in addressing in-stock levels, customer service and store traffic."

S. S. Kresge

Born: July 31, 1867
Bald Mount, Pennsylvania
Died: October 18, 1966
East Stroudsburg, Pennsylvania
Entrepreneur and philanthropist

S. S. Kresge.
Reproduced by permission of Corbis Corporation (Bellevue).

S. S. Kresge worked hard, spent his money only when necessary, and saved it wisely. This penny-pinching attitude, which began early in life, led him to become an extremely successful businessman and a generous multimillionaire. It was also the attitude shared by millions of cost-conscious customers who flocked to the five-and-dime stores and Kmart discount stores that were launched by the man himself.

"I think I was successful because I saved and because I heeded good advice ... I worked—and I didn't work only eight hours a day, but sometimes 18 hours. When one starts at the bottom and learns to scrape, then everything becomes easy."

Hard Work Pays Off

Sebastian Spering Kresge was born on July 31, 1867, in Bald Mount, Pennsylvania. His parents, Sebastian and Catherine Kunkle Kresge, were farmers of Swiss ancestry. Sebastian Jr. was given farm chores to do as early as age five. After attending schools in rural areas, he went to Fairview Academy in Brodheadsville, Pennsylvania. Kresge was so anxious to continue his schooling, he made a deal with his father: if his father paid his way through business college, Kresge agreed to give all of his earnings to his father until he turned twenty-one. His father agreed, and Kresge attended Eastman Business College in Poughkeepsie, New York.

The earnings Kresge received came from a variety of odd jobs. He was a deliveryman and clerk in a Scranton, Pennsylvania, grocery store and a teacher in Gower's School in Monroe County, Pennsylvania. He made $22 a month as a teacher. He also worked as a beekeeper, but he kept the money he made from that job for himself. According to his 1966 *New York Times* obituary, Kresge once said, "My bees ... always reminded me that hard work, thrift, sobriety and an earnest struggle to live an upright Christian life are the first rungs of the ladder of success."

In 1889, Kresge's business savvy began to take shape. He was employed as a bookkeeper at a hardware store in Scranton and noticed that when the store allowed customers to pay with credit, not cash, they bought more items than they really needed. The store, in turn, had to delay payment of some of its bills because of this policy. Later, Kresge accepted only cash payments in his stores.

Three years later, Kresge was given his big break. His employer was impressed that instead of sitting around doing nothing during slow business, Kresge would work at odd jobs. For example, Kresge was known to clean, polish, and sell old stoves. Because he showed an ability to work hard, Kresge was promoted to traveling salesman for W. B. Bertels Sons & Company. It was his responsibility to sell hardware and tinware to the New England and North Central states. One of his customers was Frank Woolworth (1852–1919), who had opened the first chain of dime stores in 1875. Kresge sold Woolworth enough products for each of his nineteen stores. The young salesman was impressed with this central ordering practice and equally pleased because it was a cash transaction.

The Growth of Kresge Stores

After eight years working as a salesman, Kresge had saved $8,000. In 1897, he invested his entire savings in the opening of two five-and-dime stores in Detroit, Michigan, and Memphis, Tennessee, with his friend, businessman John McCrory (1860–1943). By 1907, Kresge had bought out McCrory and was on his own. He incorporated the S.S. Kresge Company and became president and chairman of the board.

Kresge was president of his company until 1925, and was known as a good manager. Although he was very careful with his own money, he was generous with his employees. Kresge was known to frequently visit his red front stores and engage in conversation with clerks and managers. From the very beginning, he offered paid sick-leave, paid holidays, profit-sharing, and pensions for employees who retired.

Although Kresge stepped down as president he stayed involved with the company, serving as chairman of the board. He kept that position until a few months before his death in 1966. Kresge was also involved with other businesses and investments. He was president of Kresge Realty Company and owned department stores, including The Fair in Chicago, Illinois; Palais Royale in Washington, D.C.; Stern Brothers in New York City; and Kresge-Newark and Steinbach-Kresge stores in New Jersey. By the end of the 1920s, he was worth more than $200 million and owned stock valued at about $30 million.

Passing It On

Raised a strict Methodist with the belief that alcohol, tobacco, and gambling were unnecessary evils, Kresge also thought it was his Christian duty to share his wealth. In 1924, to commemorate the one hundredth anniversary of his company, he contributed $1.3 million to set up the Kresge Foundation "to promote the well-being of mankind." Before he died, Kresge donated approximately $175 million to the foundation.

The Kresge Foundation, still in existence but no longer affiliated with the Kmart Corporation, has provided gifts totaling over $1.5 billion since its inception to such organizations as the Methodist Children's Home in Detroit, the YMCA, the Anti-Saloon League, and many universities and hospitals. In 1999, it was one of the twenty largest foundations in the United

 The Frugal Tycoon

Throughout his lifetime, S. S. Kresge was known as thrifty and frugal. He bragged that he never spent more than thirty cents on lunch, wore inexpensive, plain suits until they practically fell apart, and lined his shoes with paper after the soles wore out. At the age of fifty-eight, Kresge was coaxed into taking up golf, but he soon quit because he lost too many balls and decided he could not afford to continually replace them.

In 1897, Kresge married Anna E. Harvey. This first of three marriages ended in divorce in 1924. Later that year, he married Doris Mercer. Their divorce came four years later, and in October 1928, he wed the woman he stayed with until his death, Clara Swaine. The chief complaint from each of his wives was that he was too stingy with his money. Their divorce settlements, however, were quite generous: Kresge's first wife (and five children) received $10 million and his second wife received $3 million.

States. Kresge's grandson, Bruce Kresge, was chairman of the board and his great-granddaughter, Deborah McDowell, was also a board member.

At the age of eighty-five, in one of his more noteworthy speeches, Kresge chose his words as wisely and frugally as he spent his money. The occasion was the dedication of Harvard University's Kresge Hall in 1953, and the speech consisted of only six words: "I never made a dime talking." Thirteen years later, in 1966, S. S. Kresge died at his home in East Stroudsburg, Pennsylvania, at the ripe old age of ninety-nine.

For More Information

Books

Plunkett-Powell, Karen. *Remembering Woolworth's: A Nostalgic History of the World's Most Famous Five-and-Dime*. New York: St. Martin's Press, 1999.

Periodicals

Hays, Constance L. "Maybe It Was the Blue Light's Hypnotic Effect." *The New York Times* (May 30, 2002): p. 5.

"'It Doesn't Get Any Better Than This.'" *Business Week* (September 4, 2000): p. 84.

"A Kmart Special: Better Service." *Business Week* (September 4, 2000): p. 80.

"Kmart's Last Chance." *Business Week* (March 11, 2002): p. 68.

Longo, Don. "How Walmart KO'd Kmart." *Retail Merchandiser* (March, 2002): p. 5.

Naughton, Keith. "Crisis at Kmart." *Newsweek* (January 28, 2002): p. 38.

Perman, Stacy. "Attention K Martha Shoppers: Martha Stewart can decorate anything, and she rules a $150 million empire." *Time* (October 6, 1997): p. 54.

"S.S. Kresge of Store Chain Dies at 99." *New York Times* (October 19, 1966): p. 38.

Taub, Stephen. "Can Kmart Come Back Again?" *Financial World* (March 31, 1983): p. 50.

Web Sites

Kmart Corporation. [On-line] http://www.kmartcorp.com (accessed on August 15, 2002).

The Kresge Foundation. [On-line] http://www.kresge.org (accessed on August 15, 2002).

Levi Strauss & Company

1155 Battery Street, Levi's Plaza
San Francisco, California 94111
(415) 501-6000
www.levistrauss.com

In 1873, Western miners began buying a new kind of work pants made by Levi Strauss & Company. The rugged pants, made from blue denim, were called "waist high overalls"; today they are known as blue jeans or simply Levi's, and they are an international symbol of American freedom and casual style.

Thanks to the popularity of its blue jeans, Levi Strauss & Company became the world's largest manufacturer of brand-name apparel. The company branched out and sold other clothes, but blue jeans remained its most famous product, and Levi's is still one of the most recognized brands in the world. Levi Strauss & Company is also hailed for its commitment to social causes and fair treatment of its workers.

Roots in the Gold Rush

In 1848, gold was discovered just outside Sacramento, California, which unleashed the first "gold rush." Tens of thousands of people from around the world descended on northern California, hoping to make a fortune mining gold. San Francisco turned into the commercial heart of the region, and its

Levi Strauss at a Glance

- **Employees:** 17,000

- **CEO:** Philip Marineau

- **Major Competitors:** VF Corp; Gap, Inc.; Tommy Hilfiger; Polo Ralph Lauren; Liz Claiborne

- **Notable Product Lines:** 501 Blue Jeans; Vintage Blue Jeans; Engineered Blue Jeans; Superlow Blue Jeans; Dockers; Slates

population grew from a few hundred to seventy thousand in just a few years. In 1853, Levi Strauss, like thousands of others, moved to the boom town of San Francisco. He planned to make his money in dry goods, selling cloth, sewing materials, and ready-made clothes.

Strauss set up his first shop near the waterfront and formed a partnership with his brother-in-law, David Stern, who was married to his sister Fanny. The enterprise was officially named Levi Strauss & Company in 1863. By then, the company sold a wider range of items, including blankets and women's clothes. Customers could also shop from a catalog.

One product Strauss sold was work pants made out of canvas. He hired tailors to make the pants for him in their homes. Later, he switched to denim as the fabric for these pants. This type of cotton cloth was known for its strength and was often dyed blue. With the success of its pants and other products, the company opened a new headquarters on Battery Street in 1866.

The Original Levi's

In 1872, a Nevada tailor named Jacob Davis asked Strauss to join him in a business venture. He had added metal rivets to the pockets of denim pants, making them less likely to rip at the seams. Seeing the value of the rivets, Strauss agreed to work with Davis. The next year, Strauss's company sold its first blue denim pants with rivets, the original Levi's blue jeans. The pants also featured two rows of V-shaped orange stitching on the back pockets, so customers could easily pick out Strauss's jeans. That "V" is still used on Levi's.

As sales grew, Levi Strauss & Company opened its first factories. At the time, many San Franciscans were upset that local companies were hiring Chinese immigrants, who would accept lower wages than American workers. Wanting to avoid any trouble with customers, Strauss hired American women to

Timeline

1853: Levi Strauss begins selling dry goods in San Francisco, California.

1873: Levi Strauss & Company sells its first pair of riveted blue jeans.

1912: Koveralls, a denim playsuit for children, is the first company product sold nationally.

1935: Levi Strauss & Company introduces its first ladies' blue jeans.

1955: Zippers appear on Levi's jeans for the first time.

1974: Company sales reach $1 billion.

1981: Robert Grohman becomes the first CEO of Levi Strauss & Company with no relation to the company's founder.

1985: After selling shares to the public for fourteen years, Levi Strauss once again becomes a private company.

1986: Levi Strauss & Company introduces Dockers, a line of casual clothes.

2001: Company officials pay more than $46,000 for a pair of Levi's more than one hundred years old.

work in his factories. He had to pay higher wages than the companies that used Chinese workers, so Levi pants cost more. To make up for the higher price, the company offered a higher-quality product. The company began promising that the pants would not rip, offering a new pair if they ever did.

The blue jeans were popular with miners and ranchers, and sales of Levi Strauss's other dry goods also rose. In 1890, Levi Strauss & Company became a corporation, issuing shares of the company to employees and members of the Strauss and Stern families. Strauss's nephews, the sons of Fanny and David Stern, now ran most of the company's business. They took complete control in 1902, after Strauss's death.

Growing Years

In 1906, a huge earthquake and the fires that followed it destroyed large parts of San Francisco. The earthquake dealt

Denim was similar to jean, another nineteenth-century cloth sometimes used to make work pants and other clothes. Over time, customers began referring to Levi Strauss's denim pants as "jeans" or "blue jeans." By 1960, Levi Strauss & Company also adopted the name.

a blow to Levi Strauss & Company, as it lost its headquarters and factories. The company quickly rebuilt, and in 1912 it introduced its first significant new product: Koveralls, denim playsuits for children. The Koveralls became the first company product sold across the United States. At the time, Levi's jeans were sold only in the West.

Despite the success of Koveralls, however, company profits started to fall after World War I (1914–18). In 1921, company president Sigmund Stern gave his son-in-law, Walter Haas, more responsibility at Levi Strauss. Haas made changes in the company's accounting and pricing practices and modernized the manufacturing process to try to improve finances. By 1928, Haas was running the entire company, and profits were up from their earlier lows.

As other U.S. companies did, Levi Strauss struggled to remain profitable during the Great Depression of the 1930s. Sales were finally boosted by a growing interest in the West and the lifestyle of cowboys. "Dude ranches" became popular, offering Easterners a vacation that featured horseback riding and living like a ranch hand. The tourists saw cowboys wearing Levi's. Western movies also showed cowboys wearing blue jeans, stirring more interest in the pants. Levi Strauss took advantage of this growing fascination with the West and began featuring cowboys in its ads. The cowboys had an image of being strong and independent. Wearing Levi's jeans, the company suggested, gave customers those qualities. Wearing Levi's blue jeans also became a popular fad among some West Coast college students.

The company's pants, however, were in short supply after 1941, when the United States entered World War II (1939–45). The U.S. government wanted denim work clothes for employees in the defense industry, and the Navy provided sailors with Levi Strauss's denim as well. When the war ended, Levi Strauss found a new market for its blue jeans. Veterans going to college for the first time boosted their popularity on campuses across the country, showing that the pants were casual clothes suited for any environment.

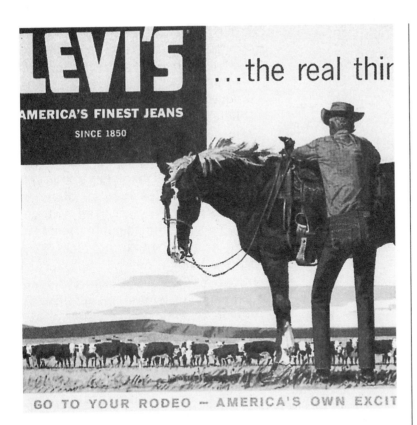

GO TO YOUR RODEO — AMERICA'S OWN EXCIT

A New Demand

In 1950, the company ended its general dry-goods business to focus on making its own denim clothes. During the "baby boom" years after World War II, when returning soldiers began raising families, Levi Strauss's advertising focused on young people. Up-and-coming movie stars of the 1950s, including Marlon Brando (1924–) and James Dean (1931–1955), made wearing Levi's "cool." The characters they portrayed in films often defied the law or adults, and blue jeans became a symbol of rebellion against authority. By the 1960s, when many young people protested racial inequality and the Vietnam War (1959–75), blue jeans were part of the "uniform" of American youth. The power of U.S. media, especially television and film, then helped spread Levi's popularity around the world.

In 1958, Walter Haas Jr. took control of Levi Strauss & Company. During his presidency the company introduced new products designed to appeal to the youth market. White jeans and pre-shrunk blue jeans appeared in 1960. Corduroy pants

A Caring Company

The Levi Strauss & Company's reputation for treating employees well began after the 1906 San Francisco earthquake. The company continued to pay all its workers as it rebuilt its factory and offices. Later, during the Great Depression (1929–34), the company kept workers busy putting in new floors in one of its factories, rather than fire them during difficult times. Levi Strauss has also taken the lead on many social issues. During the 1940s, it desegregated its factories, bringing white and African American workers together before many other industries took this step. During the early 1980s, Levi Strauss became involved in educating Americans about AIDS. The company was also one of the first to offer health benefits to workers' partners as well as to husbands or wives. Later, it led the effort to ensure that the international partners of U.S. clothing companies treated their workers fairly.

first appeared in 1963, and in 1968 the company launched a complete line of women's clothing (its first blue jeans for women had appeared in 1935). Levi's bell-bottom jeans hit the market in 1969. The basic Levi's blue jeans, however, remained the most popular item in the company's line.

In 1971, Levi Strauss sold shares to the public for the first time. It licensed the Levi's name to other clothing companies, which put the brand on such items as shoes and socks. The demand for blue jeans was so strong the company sometimes faced a shortage of denim. In 1973, however, profits fell because of some poor decisions made in the company's European division. Customers wanted bell-bottoms, but Strauss had made straight-legged pants for the market. But even with this setback, company sales reached $1 billion in 1974.

Difficulties in Changing Time

By 1977, Levi Strauss was the world's largest clothing manufacturer. Two years later, it grew again with its purchase of Koracorp, which made men's and women's sportswear. The company, however, began to face challenges in the blue jeans market, as well-known clothing designers such as Calvin Klein (1942–) began selling jeans with their names on the label. These "designer jeans" ate into Strauss's sales, and by the early 1980s profits were falling. In 1981, Robert Grohman took over as chief executive officer (CEO), marking the first time the company was led by someone without ties to the Strauss family. Grohman could not turn the company around, and Robert Haas, son of Walter Haas Jr., took control in 1984.

Haas wanted to restore the old ways of doing business. One of his first moves was to take the company private—family

The rivets that were used to keep the jeans together were one of the marks of Levi Strauss quality. They were later blunted to make sure they wouldn't scratch things such as horse saddles and wooden furniture. *Reproduced by permission of The Advertising Archive.*

members and a few executives bought all of Levi Strauss & Company's shares. Haas also sold off some of the companies Levi Strauss had bought during its growth years. In 1986, the company introduced a new line of casual pants, Dockers, that sold well, and international sales of blue jeans remained strong.

But overall profits slumped again in the early 1990s, as the company failed to adapt to fashion trends. "Hip hop" styles,

During the 1930s, Levi Strauss made some changes to its pants. The rivets on the rear pocket were covered so they wouldn't scratch saddles or chairs. The company also put a small red tag with "Levi's" on the right rear pocket, so customers could easily identify the brand.

In 2001, the company paid more than $46,000 for a pair of Levi's that sold for about $1 when they were made more than one hundred years before. The company had already launched its Vintage line, featuring reproductions of pants the company sold in the past.

made popular by many rap singers, featured baggy pants with wide legs and deep pockets. Levi Strauss, however, continued to market its traditional styles of blue jeans. The company also lost ground to major retailers, such as J. C. Penney, which began selling their own brands of jeans.

Haas continued to make changes in the company's structure and its product line. In 1996, he and a few senior managers bought out stock owned by some Haas family members and employees. That same year, Levi Strauss introduced a line of dress clothes, Slates.

Another change came in 1999, when Haas turned over the company's leadership to Philip Marineau. Strauss also tried stirring sales among teens, especially girls. In 2001, ads for Levi's Superlow jeans featured singing belly buttons, created with computer animation. Another ad campaign used the slogan "Make Them Your Own," trying to remind customers that Levi's were for people who wanted to assert their independence and unique personality. Company officials remained confident that Levi's would endure as one of the world's great brand names.

Levi Strauss

Born: February 26, 1829
Buttenheim, Germany
Died: September 26, 1902
San Francisco, California
Founder, Levi Strauss & Company

Levi Strauss.
Reproduced by permission of The Granger Collection, New York.

"I am a bachelor, and I fancy on that account I need to work more, for my entire life is my business."

Levi Strauss's life is one of the great examples of the American immigrant success story. Through hard work, the willingness to take risks, and some luck, Strauss became one of the most prominent citizens of San Francisco at the end of the nineteenth century. Strauss also lent his name to one of the best-known and best-loved U.S. products: Levi's blue jeans.

Learning the Business

Levi Strauss—first known as Loeb—was born on February 26, 1829, in the small village of Buttenheim, in the Bavarian region of Germany. His father Hirsch had four children with a first wife, and three with Rebecca Haas, Strauss's mother. The elder Strauss sold dry goods, and several of his sons continued the family business after they left Germany. The Strausses were Jewish, and the United States offered them greater freedom and opportunities.

Levi Strauss made the voyage across the Atlantic Ocean in 1847 with his mother and two sisters. After his arrival in New York, Strauss went into business with his half-brothers Jonas and Louis, who had immigrated earlier. As an employee at J. Strauss Brother & Company, Strauss learned how to buy and sell cloth and other dry goods. In 1849, Strauss left for Kentucky to work as a peddler, selling an assortment of items out of a pack or trunk he carried on his back.

By this time, gold had been discovered at Sutter's Mill, just outside Sacramento, California, drawing thousands of fortune hunters to the area. As the "gold rush" continued, Strauss's sister Fanny and her husband David Stern went to San Francisco to open a dry-goods business. In 1853, Strauss decided to join them. After becoming a U.S. citizen, he sailed for California, bringing dry goods supplied by his brothers' company.

Early Success

Strauss set up his own wholesale business, called simply Levi Strauss, and acted as the West Coast agent for his half-brothers. As his business grew, Strauss moved several times to larger quarters. Eventually David Stern joined his business. Their supplies came by ship, and the partners never knew what goods would be available. The items Strauss and Stern bought included denim work pants or the fabric itself. Most of their goods were sold to miners, but as more families came to San Francisco, Strauss and Stern added clothing for women and children. Strauss occasionally left the city to sell goods to the small shops opening up near mining camps. He developed a reputation for selling quality goods at a fair price.

By 1861, Strauss had one of the most successful dry-goods businesses in San Francisco, and the firm continued to grow. Goods still came from the New York branch of the company, but Strauss also had items made on the West Coast, including pants. The first work pants he sold were made of canvas, but Strauss later switched to denim. He hired tailors to make the pants in their homes. The pants were just one of many products sold by Levi Strauss & Company.

During these years, Strauss lived with Fanny and David Stern. Dressed formally for work, he walked each day to his office. At the company, however, Strauss was not formal with his workers, insisting they call him Levi. Strauss was also becoming a leader in San Francisco's Jewish community. He joined an organization that helped needy Jews in the region, and he helped raise money to build a temple and a cemetery.

The Pants with the Rivets

One of Strauss's customers was a Nevada tailor named Jacob Davis. Like Strauss, Davis was a Jewish immigrant. In 1872, he sent Strauss a letter describing improvements he had made to denim pants; how he had made the seams stronger near the pockets and the fly. Davis also asked Strauss to pay for an application to patent the pants. By securing a patent, no other company could use Davis's design. Strauss could see that Davis had made valuable improvements, so he readily agreed. In 1873, his company sold its first pair of blue denim pants with rivets—the original Levi's blue jeans.

To make the pants that he called "waist high overalls," Strauss opened his first manufacturing plant, with Davis supervising the operation. The company also made denim jackets with rivets and later added work shirts to its line. Within a few years, the company had several hundred workers. Although Strauss also continued to sell wholesale dry goods, making and selling his own clothes eventually became the most successful part of his business.

As Levi Strauss & Company grew, the management changed. David Stern died in 1874, and his sons—Strauss's nephews—began entering the business and taking on more responsibilities. Strauss, however, continued to make major company decisions. Strauss's fortune also grew: an 1877 report said he was worth more than $4 million. This fortune included real estate as well as his share of Levi Strauss & Company. Other companies recognized his prominence, and Strauss was asked to sit on the board of directors of several area firms. He also served on the San Francisco Board of Trade, which promoted local products.

Final Years

During the 1890s, Strauss briefly turned his attention from clothes and invested in railroads. In 1891, he and other

Even though Jacob Davis and Levi Strauss patented their riveted pants, competitors illegally copied the design. In 1874, Strauss filed the first of many lawsuits to stop other companies from copying his blue jeans.

The Haas Family Takes Charge

With no children to run Levi Strauss & Company after his death, Levi Strauss left his business to his nephews, the Sterns. In 1919, Jacob Stern brought his son-in-law Walter Haas into the company. Haas became chief executive officer (CEO) in 1928, and he and his sons receive the credit for making Levi Strauss & Company a worldwide leader in the apparel industry.

Walter Haas Sr. was born in San Francisco in 1889. He graduated from the University of California, Berkeley, in 1910 after majoring in business. After serving in the military during World War I (1914–18), Haas took a job at Levi Strauss & Company. Within a few years, Haas asked his brother-in-law, Daniel Koshland, to join the firm. The two men focused on ways to improve profits at the company.

Haas served as CEO until 1955, then remained as chairman of the board until 1970. He remained active in the company's affairs until his death in 1979. His sons, Walter J. and Peter, were also heavily involved in the company. Haas Jr., like his father, studied business at Berkeley. He thought about being a doctor, but Levi Strauss was still a small company when Haas left college in 1937, and he felt compelled to enter the family business. He attended Harvard Business School and then joined Levi Strauss as a stock boy. In 1958, he succeeded Daniel Koshland as CEO. With Haas Jr. running the company, Levi Strauss began to grow tremendously. "I don't think anybody could have anticipated the jeans boom [of the 1960s]," he told *Daily News Record*. Haas Jr. stepped down as CEO in 1976, and his brother took over.

In 1980, Haas Jr. won the respect of San Francisco Bay area residents when he bought the Oakland A's baseball team. The team likely would have left Oakland if he had not stepped in. Haas Jr., like his father, was also famous for his generosity. Both men gave large sums to Berkeley; the business school there is named for Haas Sr. Both also started foundations to distribute some of their wealth to charitable causes. An obituary after the younger Haas's death in 1995 noted that that he often said his generosity was "in the genes."

Haas Jr.'s son Robert took over Levi Strauss & Company in 1984. He continued the family tradition of attending Berkeley and, like his father, graduated from the Harvard Business School. Haas also served in the Peace Corps and worked as a consultant before joining the family business in 1973. Under Robert Haas, Levi Strauss & Company saw its best year ever in 1996, when sales reached $7.1 billion. After that, however, sales fell, and in 1999 Haas brought in Philip Marineau, the former CEO of Pepsi North America (see **PepsiCo, Inc.** entry), to run the company. Marineau was only the second person without ties to Levi Strauss to run the company. Haas remained involved with the company as the chairman of the board.

San Francisco merchants wanted to open their own railway to combat the high prices charged by existing lines to ship goods. That plan failed. A few years later, Strauss invested $25,000 in another railroad plan. This time, the man behind the project sold all the shares to another railroad company, which then struck a deal with the existing firms that charged high fares. After that disappointment, Strauss gave up on railroads and stuck with the business he knew best.

In 1897, Strauss again turned to philanthropy, giving money to the University of California, Berkeley, to fund twenty-eight scholarships. Strauss realized that having a fortune brought with it a responsibility to share. In an 1895 interview quoted in *Everyone Wears His Name,* Strauss said that riches "do not cause happiness to their owners." Spreading the wealth, he believed, brought greater joy.

By 1902, illness began to slow down Strauss, and he took a vacation to try to restore his health. By fall, however, his condition worsened, and he died in his sleep during the night of September 26. His death made the headlines of local papers, and shopkeepers closed their businesses to attend his funeral. Today, the Levi Strauss & Company Web site notes that its founder was praised for "his broad and generous love for and sympathy with humanity." He also left behind his name on the pants that became an American classic decades after his death.

For More Information

Books

Henry, Sondra, and Emily Taitz. *Levi Strauss: Everyone Wears His Name.* Minneapolis: Dillon Press, 1990.

Periodicals

Emert, Carol. "Levi Strauss Hires New CEO from Outside Its Gene Pool." *San Francisco Chronicle* (September 8, 1999): p. A1.

"Longtime Levi Strauss & Company leader Walter A. Haas, Jr., Dies." *Business Wire* (September 20, 1995).

Marion, Peggy. "Walter Haas: Levi's Crusader." *Daily News Record* (November 7, 1983): p. 12.

Munk, Nina. "How Levi's Trashed a Great American Brand." *Fortune* (April 12, 1999): p. 82.

Norton, Justin M.. "Levi's Takes 'Low' Road with Soprano as Singer." *Brandweek* (June 18, 2001): p. 6.

Rhine, John. "Levi Rips the World's Oldest Jeans to Market." *San Francisco Business Times* (June 29, 2001): p. 6.

Sherman, Stratford. "Levi's As Ye Sew, So Shall Ye Reap." *Fortune* (May 17, 1997): p. 104.

Web Sites

Haas School of Business, University of California at Berkeley. [On-line] http://www.haas.berkeley.edu/haas/about.html (accessed on August 15, 2002).

Levi Strauss & Company. [On-line] http://www.levistrauss.com (accessed on August 15, 2002).

L.L. Bean, Inc.

15 Casco Street
Freeport, ME 04033
(800) 221-4221
www.llbean.com

L. L. Bean, Inc., an award-winning American mail-order and clothing retailer, was founded over ninety years ago as a sportsmen's outfitter, selling waterproof boots for hunters. Over the years the company expanded into over three hundred product categories for men, women, children, pets, and the home—all with an ironclad guarantee. As the world's leading mail-order business, L.L. Bean's label stands not only for high quality, durable products, but for the satisfaction of each and every one of its customers.

A Love of the Outdoors

Leon Leonwood Bean (known as "L. L.") was born and raised in Maine. After his parents died, he lived with relatives in different parts of the state until he ventured out on his own. Although his education only went as far as the eighth grade, he later took business courses at local colleges and used this knowledge to earn a living. A lifelong lover of the outdoors, Bean often relied on his hunting and fishing skills to provide food. He married in 1898, fathered three children, and over the

L.L. Bean at a Glance

- **Employees:** 4,700 (increases during winter months to more than 9,000)

- **CEO:** Chris McCormick

- **Subsidiaries:** L.L. Bean stores; L.L. Bean outlets; L.L. Kids

- **Major Competitors:** American Eagle Outfitters; Bass Pro Shops; Coldwater Creek; Eddie Bauer, Inc.; J. Crew; Lands' End

- **Notable Products:** Bean Boot (formerly Maine Hunting Shoe); Bean's Classic Porch Rocker; Boat & Tote Bags; Burrito Bag (sleeping bag); Maine Cedar Outdoor Furniture; Photo Essentials apparel line (for photographers); Water Hogs (outdoor/indoor mats)

next decade or so struggled to support his family.

As a hunter, Bean traveled in the woods in all kinds of weather and tired of always having wet, cold feet. In 1911, he decided to do something about it. He designed a sturdy boot and took the to a local shoemaker. Leather was used for the top and side parts of the boot and a thick rubber-soled bottom was added to keep feet dry and warm. The boot was called the "Maine Hunting Shoe." Pleased with the design's initial success, Bean formed a company in 1912, using his own name, to sell the boots to other hunters and fishermen in the area. Using mailing lists from the state hunting board, he mailed three-page flyers to men who had applied for Maine hunting licenses. He soon received several orders, and the L.L. Bean mail-order company was in business.

Within months, the new company faced its first crisis. Customers complained that their shoes fell apart and water leaked in. Rather than ignore the problems, Bean offered his customers a full refund. He then reworked the boots with help from a Boston rubber company and contacted his original buyers, telling them about the improved boot. Bean's insistence that he must provide clients with only the highest quality proved invaluable to the small company. It was the beginning of L.L. Bean's world famous promise: satisfaction was absolutely guaranteed, no matter what, or all money was refunded.

Over the next several years, business grew steadily and a variety of recreational clothes and footwear was introduced. With the increase in sales, Bean was able to expand his one-room operation to open a manufacturing plant and office in downtown Freeport, Maine, in 1917. He then applied for both United States and Canadian patents on the hunting boot, to protect his design from imitators.

 **Timeline**

1911: Maine Hunting Shoe is developed by Leon Leonwood Bean.

1912: L.L. Bean is formed in Freeport, Maine.

1917: Manufacturing plant and office opens on Main Street in Freeport.

1920: Main Street store opens.

1924: Employees number twenty-four; sales top $130,000.

1937: Sales reach $1 million.

1941: Company designs and sells boots to the military during World War II.

1951: Employees total over one hundred; Main Street store now open twenty-four hours a day.

1960: Bean's grandson, Leon Gorman, joins the family business.

1967: Founder Leon L. Bean dies and Leon Gorman becomes CEO.

1992: L.L. Bean enters partnership with Japanese companies.

1993: L.L. Kids is introduced.

1995: Company receives 150,000 orders per day; sales hit $4.5 million.

1996: On-line shopping service is launched.

1999: Sales climb to over $1 billion.

2000: Second L.L. Bean store opens in Maclean, Virginia.

2001: Third store opens in Columbia, Maryland; Chris McCormick becomes CEO.

Location, Location, Location

A key factor to L.L. Bean's early success was the company's location. Perched atop Freeport's post office, Bean could pack up his shipments and walk downstairs to mail them. With the introduction of the parcel post rate in 1912, small packages could be shipped anywhere in the United States quite cheaply. An added plus was that Bean's brother was Freeport's postmaster.

By the 1920s, L.L. Bean was earning a reputation among sportsmen as the best outfitter for camping, hiking, hunting,

A shoemaker works on the leather uppers of L.L. Bean's famous Maine Hunting Shoe at the company's shoe factory in Freeport, Maine.
Reproduced by permission of Corbis Corporation (Bellevue).

and fishing. In addition to a wide range of sturdy apparel, the company also began selling equipment, including canoes, tents, and fishing rods. The items were sold through the L.L. bean catalog or in the company store, which opened on Main Street in 1920. Bean's little mail-order company was a hit in Freeport and beyond, and the firm employed two dozen full-time workers by 1924.

L.L. Bean continued to grow and expand in the 1930s, with Bean writing and producing the company's well-known scrapbook-styled catalog. Featuring descriptive paragraphs written in Bean's folksy tone, his genuine love for the outdoors and L.L. Bean products came through on every page. The cover of the catalog always included an outdoor scene, painted by local and later famous artists who wanted to be a part of the L.L. Bean legend. By 1937, sales had reached a phenomenal $1 million.

World War II and Beyond

With the United States embroiled in World War II (1939–45), L.L. Bean contributed to the war effort by designing and manufacturing boots for the country's servicemen overseas. Different boot models, all based on the company's original waterproof Maine Hunting Shoe, were shipped to military posts. After the victorious end of the war in 1945, America was a happy, prosperous place, with growing families spending more than ever on recreational goods.

By the beginning of the 1950s, the L.L. Bean store on Main Street was open twenty-four hours a day and the company employed one hundred people to service customers whenever they might need a fishing lure, waterproof boot, or hunting license. These patrons, mostly men but also a growing number of women, helped the company's sales climb to

$2 million in 1951. To address the increasing number of its women fans, L.L. Bean created a department just for them in 1954.

The 1960s ushered in a new age for L.L. Bean when grandson Leon Gorman joined the family business. Bean was in his late eighties, and although he had slowed down and was somewhat retired, he was still very involved in the company and the 100-page catalog bearing his name. Yet the aging founder knew it was time to groom his successor, and he chose young Gorman who had been taught well by Bean and his brother Carl (who had been helping run the company). Gorman took the reins of a company bringing in $4 million in annual sales the year his grandfather died in 1967.

> L. Bean offers a multitude of programs and activities so that employees can become experienced and knowledgeable about the outdoors. Programs include Fly Fishing School, which is a three-day course, and three yearly "outdoor experience days."

A New Era

Although Gorman respected his grandfather's style of conducting business (such as never firing an employee or agonizing over failed products), he believed it was time to take L.L. Bean into the twentieth century. This meant applying the many technological advances that had become available and expanding into other areas, which his grandfather had not always favored. Leon senior had made all the money he needed, lived comfortably, and had often told his grandson, "I eat three meals a day, I can't eat four." Yet to compete with its growing rivals, L.L. Bean needed to flex its outdoorsy muscles.

While L.L. Bean was never considered fashionable, it did hold a certain elitist charm for its many loyal customers, who spent more than $30 million a year on Bean merchandise. To them, L.L. Bean meant the best of the best for their pursuits, providing warmth, durability, and practicality. Younger generations had long found the firm's apparel the opposite of fashionable, and so it was with some surprise that L.L. Bean was awarded the prestigious Coty American Fashion Critics Award in 1975. The commendation was not only a tribute to the company's enduring popularity but marked a resurgence of the old-fashioned, down-to-earth kind of fashion that had always been

L. L. Bean's grandson, Leon Gorman.

Reproduced by permission of AP/Wide World Photos.

L.L. Bean's image. Many of the people who had mocked L.L. Bean's folksy appeal now embraced it as mainstream style.

By the beginning of the 1980s, L.L. Bean sales were $140 million and mushroomed to $250 million by 1984. When the firm celebrated its seventy-fifth anniversary in 1987, not only was the L.L. Bean catalog still the mainstay of the company, with over seventy-five million copies mailed to customers annually, but the Main Street store had become a true tourist destination attracting some two million visitors every year to see the six thousand products displayed from wall to wall. Sales for 1987 surpassed $360 million, with nearly two thousand workers taking orders and selling merchandise.

An important part of L.L. Bean's continuing success was its willingness to both sell and repair its merchandise, most especially its updated Maine Hunting Shoe, which became known as the Bean Boot. Customers could have their boots resoled for half the price of a new pair, and the firm repaired and shipped more than sixteen thousand pairs a year by the end of the decade.

Trouble in Paradise

As the 1990s got underway, L.L. Bean was suffering from falling sales, soaring postage costs, and high returns. The once mighty retailer was considered dull compared to its competitors, which included Lands' End, Patagonia, and **Eddie Bauer, Inc.** (see entry). With newcomers crowding the outdoor and recreational market, the rustic L.L. Bean lacked the glamor and youthful appeal of its rivals, who spent millions on hip advertising in newspapers and magazines and on television.

In response to sluggish sales, the company was forced to lay off some of its thirty-five hundred employees and stop production on a new manufacturing plant in Hampden, Maine. Yet Gorman was determined to turn things around. By 1992, he had installed new state-of-the-art equipment in the company's warehouses and factories, introduced more than two dozen "specialty" catalogs, remodeled the Main Street store into a huge three-story landmark, and formed partnerships with the Japanese, who were big L.L. Bean fans, to open new stores.

L.L. Bean made several moves in the middle and late 1990s to ensure its future against rivals Lands' End and Eddie Bauer. In 1993, the company launched L.L. Kids with apparel and sports equipment for children. It also expanded its women's line, started a company Web site in 1995, and introduced an on-line shopping service in 1996. While the earliest Web site offered little more than product descriptions, it evolved into an informational site that featured over a thousand products, and offered background on the company, outdoor tips, and even a travel directory for national parks.

Over the years, scores of the rich and famous confessed to being L.L. Bean fanatics, including such notables as diplomat Eleanor Roosevelt (1884–1962), author Ernest Hemingway (1899–1961), and baseball great Babe Ruth (1895–1948).

L.L. Bean Approaching One Hundred Years

By the twenty-first century, L.L. Bean had changed its image and embarked on risky expansion. In addition to its

Waterproof "duck" boots sit on a bench in the fitting area of the shoe department in the Freeport, Maine, L.L. Bean store.
Reproduced by permission of Corbis Corporation (Bellevue).

original Freeport store, a second retail store opened in Maclean, Virginia, and a third in Columbia, Maryland, along with several outlet stores. There were plans to open additional retail stores in the north and eastern parts of the United States, to give customers more of a chance to see L.L. Bean products up close. "We've seen catalog companies expanding into retail over the past few years," Stephen Berman, an analyst at Kurt Salmon Associates told *Women's Wear Daily* back in June 1999. "It's an opportunity and a vehicle for those businesses to reach additional customers who aren't necessarily comfortable not touching and feeling the merchandise." L.L. Bean was following the same formula in Japan, where the number of retail shops had grown to twenty.

In addition to opening more stores, L.L. Bean lent its name to something entirely different: a sports utility vehicle (SUV). Forming a partnership with Subaru, the new Outback Special L.L. Bean Edition SUV hit the road in 2000 and was competing with Eddie Bauer's Limited Edition Ford Explorers and

Expeditions (see **Ford Motor Company** entry). Other new directions included launching the L.L. Bean Home Collection and women's skin-care line.

Along with new product launches and a spiffier image came a new CEO in 2001. After thirty-four years of running the company, Leon Gorman turned L.L. Bean over to a non-family member, Chris McCormick. "The family is comfortable with Chris," Gorman told the *Boston Globe* in May 2001. "The core traditions of L.L. Bean are in good hands." Gorman remained chairman of the board, while McCormick handled the duties of chief executive and president.

McCormick had been with L.L. Bean for eighteen years and was well qualified to carry on the firm's long tradition of filling the needs of the outdoor and leisure markets. One thing, however, would never change: the L.L. Bean unconditional guarantee. Customer service would always reign supreme at L.L. Bean.

L.L. Bean has been known to personally deliver items promised for Christmas or special occasions. In 1996, an entire Federal Express 747 airplane was filled with late-arriving toboggans and flown around the country to ensure that kids received them before Christmas day.

L. L. Bean

**Born: November 13, 1872
Greenwood, Maine
Died: February 5, 1967
Pompano Beach, Florida
Founder, L. L. Bean, Inc.**

"Sell good merchandise at a reasonable profit, treat your customers like human beings, and they will always come back for more."—"L. L.'s Golden Rule," from the L.L. Bean Web site

L.L. Bean is a name recognized around the world, but not everyone knows there was a real person behind it. Leon Leonwood Bean, known as "L. L.", started a small mail-order business in 1912 to sell a waterproof hunting boot of his own design. Bean and his namesake business went on to become the world's largest mail-order company, sending out millions of catalogs a year and eventually branching out into several stores and outlets in the United States and Japan. From humble beginnings to its status as an internationally known corporation, the L.L. Bean company is still family owned, with founder Bean's grandson serving as chairman.

Doing What It Takes

Leon Leonwood Bean was born in Greenwood, Maine, in 1872, one of six children. He was orphaned at the age of twelve when his parents, Benjamin and Sarah Bean, died within a short time of each other. He and his four brothers and sister were taken in by relatives in South Paris, Maine. A few years later, young Bean moved to West Minot, Maine, to live with an uncle.

As a young man, Bean loved the outdoors and was an avid hunter and fisherman. After he finished the eighth grade, his traditional schooling ended. His later education consisted of a few business courses at area colleges in the early 1890s. In 1898, Bean married Bertha Porter and worked at various jobs to support his family, including selling soap and making dairy products. He and Bertha eventually had three children, and traveled around northeastern Maine as Bean looked for steady work.

The Beans eventually settled in Freeport, a small town on Maine's eastern coast, near Portland. Leon and brother Ervin opened a dry-goods store, run mostly by Ervin while Leon spent the majority of his time outdoors. His frustration over wet, cold feet prompted him to design a waterproof boot with leather uppers and a rubber sole in 1911. After a nearby shoemaker stitched the leather to the rubber for him, Bean decided to sell the boots through the mail to men who had purchased hunting licenses in Maine. Using the state's mailing list, he put together a short, descriptive pamphlet with an order form for his invention, the Maine Hunting Shoe.

Bean eventually received about one hundred orders for the Maine Hunting Shoe, and happily mailed them out to his customers. Unfortunately, some of the stitching came undone and others cracked, so ninety of the customers wrote him back and expressed their disappointment. Disheartened and ashamed, Bean offered full refunds to each of his buyers and was determined to correct the problems. He borrowed money, traveled to Boston, Massachusetts, and worked with the United States Rubber Company to secure the leather uppers firmly to the rubber soles and make his boots watertight and durable. The new and improved Maine Hunting Shoe was everything Bean had promised his customers, and the L.L. Bean Company was formed in 1912.

From Boots to Booming Business

Over the next twenty-five years, Leon Bean built L.L. Bean into a thriving mail-order business famous up and down the east coast of the United States. His catalog was enjoyed by many, and thousands eagerly awaited its arrival in their mailboxes each year. By 1937, the company was bringing in sales of $1 million, and there was a small L.L. Bean manufacturing

Since the earliest days of the company, Leon Bean always personally tested each item in his catalog, which eventually included many more items than his original Maine Hunting Shoe.

plant, office, and store on Main Street in Freeport. Two years later, in 1939, Bertha Bean died. The following year Bean married for a second time, to Claire Boudreau, who would be his life-long companion.

In 1941, when the United States entered World War II (1939–45), L.L. Bean supplied the military with updated versions of its famous waterproof boots, and soldiers posted all over the world owed their dry, warm feet to Leon Bean. During this time, Bean decided to write a how-to book for his many fans. This was not a surprising feat since Bean wrote the copy for his company's catalog. Titled *Hunting, Fishing, and Camping,* the book offered tips for successful ventures into the wilderness. Published in 1942, it sold one hundred fifty thousand copies and had tear-out sections to provide handy references for its readers. It was reprinted numerous times.

Another milestone for Bean and his company came in 1951, when the Main Street store started staying open twenty-four hours a day, three hundred sixty-five days a year. Bean claimed he threw away the keys, so he had to keep the doors open. The real reason, however, was that hunters and fishermen do not keep the same hours as other folks and often needed supplies or licenses or clothing in the late evening or early morning hours before the sun rose. Bean was committed to meeting the needs of his customers—with practical, reasonably priced, and guaranteed items—no matter what time of the day or night.

Business World Loses a Country Charmer

By the 1960s, Bean was getting on in years. He still worked on his beloved catalog, styled like a scrapbook, with folksy descriptions, sometimes goofily named products, and hunting and fishing hints. While some found his style endearing, others found it old-fashioned and silly. This never deterred Bean, because he was genuinely devoted to his personally-tested merchandise and his loyal customers.

Bean built his empire on two simple principles: offer quality products with an absolute money-back guarantee and follow the "Golden Rule." The Golden Rule was all about respect and courtesy, and clearly worked: "Sell good merchandise at a reasonable profit, treat your customers like human beings, and they will always come back for more." Bean followed this rule and insisted that everyone who worked for him do the same, including his grandson Leon Gorman, who had started working at the company in 1960 as the senior Leon was spending more time away from the family business.

In honor of founder L. L. Bean's love of the wilderness, the company regularly contributes millions of dollars to such conservation groups as the Appalachian Trail Conference, Chesapeake Bay Foundation, Leave No Trace, Maine Island Trail Association, and the National Parks Foundation.

In 1960, Bean penned another book. Called *My Story: The Autobiography of a Down-East Merchant,* it describes how he went from humble beginnings to become the head of one of the most successful companies in the United States. In 1967, Bean was in Florida with his second wife Claire when he died on February 7 at the age of ninety-four.

A sportsman, businessman, and inventor, Leon Leonwood Bean had lived his life his own way, creating a legendary company that was copied by dozens of imitators. Of course, few could match L.L. Bean's country charm or the devotion of its customers. From one pair of waterproof boots came a mail-order and retail empire with sales of over $1 billion annually. The original twenty-four-hour L.L. Bean store in Freeport, Maine, still has no locks on its doors and has only closed once in its eighty-year history: the day of Leon L. Bean's funeral.

For More Information

Books

Bean, L. L. *Hunting, Fishing, and Camping.* 1942. Reprint, Bedford, MA: Applewood Books, 1993.

———. *My Story: The Autobiography of a Down-East Merchant.* Freeport, ME: L.L. Bean, 1960.

Griffin, Carlene. *Spillin' the Beans: Behind the Scenes at L.L. Bean.* Freeport, ME: L.L. Bean, 1993.

The L.L. Bean Guide to the Outdoors. New York: Random House, 1981.

Montgomery, M. R. *In Search of L.L. Bean.* New York: New American Library, 1987.

Periodicals

Berman, Phyllis. "Trouble in Bean Land." *Forbes* (July 6, 1992): p. 42.

Hays, Constance L. "L.L. Bean Casts About for Ways to Grow." *New York Times* (August 14, 1999): p. B1.

"Maine Retailer L.L. Bean Names First Outsider as CEO." *Boston Globe* (May 22, 2001): n.p.

Maxwell, Alison. "L.L. Bean to Increase Sites for Retail Stores." *Women's Wear Daily* (June 1, 1999): p. 4.

Skow, John. "Using the Old Bean." *Sports Illustrated* (December 2, 1985) p. 84.

Symonds, William C. "Paddling Harder at L.L. Bean." *Business Week* (December 7, 1998): p. 72.

Tedeschi, Bob. "L.L. Bean Stays Current by Staying Midstream." *New York Times* (September 20, 2000): p. D7.

Web Sites

L.L. Bean, Inc. [On-line] http://www.llbean.com (accessed on August 15, 2002).

Lucent Technologies

600 Mountain Avenue
Murray Hill, NJ 07974
(908) 582-8500
www.lucent.com

Talking with a friend over long distances, whether by telephone, cellular phone, or computer, has never been easier thanks to the innovations developed by ancestors of Lucent Technologies. Lucent has roots reaching back to 1876, when inventors raced to build the first telephone. It started as American Bell, combined forces with Western Electric, and then finally became American Telephone & Telegraph (AT&T). In 1996, AT&T split into three separate companies: AT&T, NCR, and Lucent. Today, Lucent remains one of the leading providers of telecommunications equipment throughout the world. And, with the help of its research and development arm, Bell Labs, it continues to develop equipment that transports voice and data in record speed.

An Historic Beginning

Alexander Graham Bell had been working on the plans for an electric telephone for several years when he submitted his designs to the United States Patent Office in January 1876. On the very same day, just a few hours later, another inventor,

Lucent at a Glance

- **Employees:** 77,000

- **CEO:** Patricia F. Russo

- **Subsidiaries:** Bell Laboratories; Agere Systems, AG; Communication Systems Corporation

- **Major Competitors:** 3Com; Alcatel; Cisco Systems; Motorola; Nokia; Nortel Networks; Tellabs; Toshiba

Elisha Gray (1835–1901), also submitted a patent application for an electric telephone. Gray was cofounder of the Western Electric Manufacturing Company, known for producing electrical equipment, typewriters, and telegraph equipment. Although Gray had been awarded seventy patents throughout his lifetime, he lost the race to become the inventor of the telephone. Alexander Graham Bell was issued the first telephone patent, No.174,465, on March 7, 1876.

After many experiments, Bell and his laboratory assistant, Thomas A. Watson (1854–1934), sent the first message using a telephone. On March 10, 1876, while Bell was in one room and Watson in another in their shop on Court Street in Boston, Massachusetts, Bell accidentally spilled a chemical and spoke the famous words, "Watson, please come here. I want you." This was the first time a complete understandable sentence was transmitted by electrical impulses through a wire.

Over the following two decades, the company responsible for developing and manufacturing telephone equipment went through several changes. In 1877, Bell, along with Watson and two other partners, formed the Bell Telephone Company. They purchased a controlling interest in Elisha Gray's Western Electric Company in 1881. In 1899, Bell changed his company's name to American Telephone & Telegraph (AT&T). In 1907, Theodore N. Vail, a former employee of the Western Union Telegraph Company, became president of AT&T and combined the Western Electric and AT&T engineering departments to form what would later be known as Bell Telephone Laboratories.

The Birth of Lucent

For most of the twentieth century, AT&T went through a series of name changes, company purchases, and breakups that would eventually lead to Lucent Technologies. Until the 1980s,

Timeline

1876: Alexander Graham Bell receives the first telephone patent.

1877: Bell Telephone Company is formed.

1881: Bell purchases a controlling interest in Western Electric Company.

1899: Bell changes company name to American Telephone & Telegraph (AT&T).

1907: Thomas N. Vail becomes president of AT&T and Bell Labs is formed.

1922: Alexander Graham Bell dies.

1937: Bell Lab scientist receives first of eleven Bell Labs Nobel Prizes.

1947: Bell Labs invents the transistor.

1958: Bell Labs invents the laser.

1960s: Bell Labs invents UNIX.

1984: AT&T divides into seven regional phone companies called "Baby Bells."

1996: AT&T splits into three companies and Lucent is born. Henry Schact is CEO.

1997: Richard McGinn is hired as Lucent's CEO.

1999: Lucent's initial public offering earns a record $3 billion.

2000: Lucent experiences a drop in stock price and revenue; company lays off thousands of employees.

2002: Patricia F. Russo becomes president and CEO of Lucent.

AT&T had been a monopoly, which means it had exclusive control of manufacturing phone equipment and long-distance telephone lines in the United States. After it refused to lease lines to long-distance companies like MCI, the United States Justice Department forced AT&T to break up into seven regional phone companies, known as "Baby Bells," in 1984.

Ten years later, the United States government deregulated, or removed restrictions from, the telecommunications industry. This means that AT&T finally had some competition. The company wanted to stay ahead of this new competition, so in 1996, they divided their corporation into three separate

In 1877, when Bell Telephone was established, there were 3,000 telephones in American homes; in 1900, the number of phones rose to 1.4 million. By the end of the twentieth century, there were phones in more than 100 million households nationwide.

companies: NCR Corporation made large computers; a new AT&T provided long-distance, wireless, and credit card services; and Lucent Technologies made telephones, network switching equipment, and computer chips. Lucent also acquired most of Bell Laboratories.

Innovations That Touch the Lives of Millions

Since 1925, scientists at Bell Labs have been credited with more than forty thousand inventions. In addition to telephone technology, Bell Labs provided Hollywood with the practical means to add sound to silent movies, and made communications and command equipment for the United States military during World War II (1939–45).

In 1947, three Bell Labs scientists received the Nobel Prize for their invention of the revolutionary transistor, an electronic device used to control the flow of electricity. Bell Labs devised the transistor to replace manual telephone exchange switches with automatic electronic switches. Before this, in order to telephone a friend, a person had to call an operator who placed the call for them using flexible cords that plugged into the correct socket, or jack, on a switchboard. So, in effect, the operator controlled the flow. The new technology also amplified long distance signals. Today, transistors exist within nearly all electronic devices such as computers, video cameras, CD players, remote controls, and cell phones.

Bell Labs continued to develop many more technological firsts. In 1958, Arthur L. Schawlow (1921–1999), a Bell Labs researcher, and Charles H. Townes (1915–), a consultant to Bell Labs, made history when they invented the laser. Originally known by the acronym LASER, meaning Light Amplification by Stimulated Emission of Radiation, billions of these intense beams of light are at work every day in areas such as manufacturing, construction, and medicine. In telecommunications, lasers transmit voice, data, and video through tiny strands of encased glass called fiber optic waveguides. For example, when an item is purchased at a grocery store it is scanned by a laser. The information from its bar code, including the price, is transmitted to the computerized cash register.

Beginning in the 1960s, transmitting information using computers became increasingly important. In response, Bell Labs scientists developed UNIX, a computer operating system that played a major role in the early days of the Internet. And, more recently, to support the billions of phone calls and the190 billion e-mail messages sent each year, Bell Labs developed technology to provide efficient and rapid movement of voice and data.

The word *lucent* dates back to the fifteenth century and means "glowing light." Lander Associates, a San Francisco design firm, came up with the name to describe the company's clarity of thought, purpose, and vision. Lucent's logo, a red, sketched circle, is called "the innovation ring."

In 2002, with sixteen thousand employees working in sixteen countries around the world, Bell Labs continues to make amazing advancements in telecommunications. For example, they are developing the world's first functional transistor that is only one molecule thick. Early transistors were about the size of a lightbulb, and actually looked like a lightbulb, with glass surrounding a metal filament. If new transistors are one molecule thick, it means that they are much thinner than a piece of paper.

The Rise and Fall of an Empire

When AT&T split into three companies in 1996, Lucent was the biggest corporate spin-off in American history. Lucent completed an initial public offering (IPO) by selling stock in itself for the first time. Sales of this stock raised $3 billion. The company was off and running, and many investors and financial specialists predicted a bright future. Henry Schact, a fifteen-year AT&T board member, was chosen to lead the way as Lucent's first chief executive officer (CEO).

For the next three years, Lucent purchased and merged with several other companies to expand their products and services. Some of the larger transactions included their $20 billion acquisition of Ascend Communications, an independent Internet supplier, and a $3.7 billion merger with service specialist

Lucent Techno Speak: What Does It All Mean?

- **Communications networking equipment:** A communications network is a system of computers, terminals, and other devices that are interconnected. Lucent makes the hardware and software that lets the parts of the system speak to each other, or exchange data. For example, counselors in a school use networked computers to share information about student schedules.

- **Internet service provider (ISP):** An ISP is a company that consumers and businesses go to for their Internet service. Lucent develops the infrastructure, or the electronic system, that helps ISPs provide Internet service. Examples of ISPs are American Online, Microsoft Network (MSN), and Comcast.

- **Optical network:** Lucent develops optical networks, which carry digitized voice or data at very high speed on multiple channels of light. Optical networks are used in Internet, video, and multimedia technology. For instance, cable television is now distributed to homes through optical networks. One result is that you can get hundreds of TV channels to surf through.

- **Wireless network:** Lucent creates networks that allow wireless devices to talk to each other. Wireless devices include cellular phones and pagers.

International Network Services. In a 1999 *New York Times* article, Robert Rich of the Yankee Group, a technology research company in Boston, said "If you are looking for one-stop shopping, Lucent will have more arrows in its quiver than anyone else." The company enjoyed steady growth until 1999 when the number of employees reached 153,000, and Lucent stockholders benefited from stock prices at $77 a share, an enormous increase from $7 a share at its IPO.

Soon, however, good times began to turn bad. "The company got off to a fast start selling equipment like switches that help carriers connect telephone calls to traditional phone companies like its former parent," said Kevin Peraino in a 2000 *Newsweek* article. The problem was, Perano went on to say, that Lucent did not keep up with the times. It did not focus enough on Internet technology. At the time the article was printed, Lucent's stock had dropped more than 70 percent.

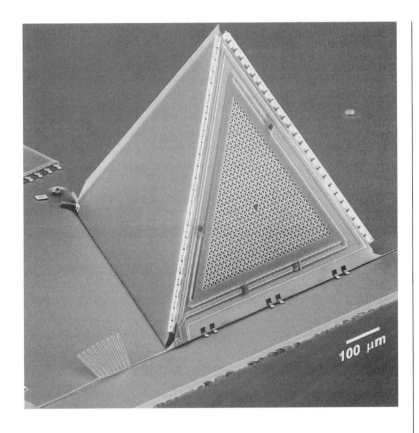

A microscopic view of a tiny microphone on a computer chip being developed by researchers at Lucent Technologies's Bell Laboratories in Murray Hill, New Jersey. The tiny pyramid-shaped microphone could lead to radio communicators the size of a wristwatch.
Reproduced by permission of AP/Wide World Photos.

Changing of the Guards

In 1997, Richard McGinn, an AT&T salesman since the 1960s, replaced Schact as CEO and chairman of Lucent. When the company began to take a downturn in 2000, Schact replaced McGinn and returned to serve as Lucent's temporary boss until a permanent replacement was found. Schact said in a 2000 *Wall Street Journal* article, "We are looking at 2001 as a transition and rebuilding year for Lucent." But its problems only got worse. By January 2002, over sixty thousand Lucent employees had been laid off, and its stock was sold at $6.94. It was time for a new leader.

On January 7, 2002, a 49-year-old resident of Trenton, New Jersey, and twenty-year company employee, Patricia F. Russo, became Lucent's new CEO, while Schact remained as chairman. "We've built a plan that is solid, credible and broad-based. And we're going to restore this company to the luster it once had," Russo told the authors of a *Wall Street Journal* article on January 8, 2002.

Lucent files an average of four patent applications each workday and has received twenty-eight thousand patents since 1925. Bell Labs researchers have been awarded eleven Nobel Prizes, with the first going to Clinton J. Davisson (1881–1958) in 1937, for his experiments on the wave nature of electrons.

Skeptics questioned Lucent's ability to bounce back unless the company's and Russo's goals stayed focused on what it does best: producing equipment for large telecommunications companies like AT&T and Verizon. David Toung, a telecommunications equipment analyst, said in a January 8, 2002, article in a Bergen County, New Jersey, newspaper, *The Record,* "I think this company will ride the telecom market and when the telecom market comes back, they will come back."

Alexander Graham Bell

Born: March 3, 1847
Edinburgh, Scotland
Died: August 2, 1922
Baddeck, Nova Scotia
Inventor and educator

Alexander Graham Bell.
Reproduced by permission of Corbis Corporation (Bellevue).

"It is possible to connect every man's house, office or factory with a central station, so as to give him direct communication with his neighbors."

Because of family tradition and upbringing, Alexander Graham Bell was, perhaps, destined to create one of the world's most commonly used inventions today: the telephone. He came from two generations of men who were students of speech and language and a hard-of-hearing mother who was a musician. These influences led him to dedicate his life to science and sound as well as to the education of the deaf.

Teacher of the Deaf

Alexander Graham Bell was born on March 3, 1847, in Edinburgh, Scotland. He was the middle of three sons born to Alexander Melville Bell and Eliza Grace Symonds. Alexander Melville's father, Alexander Bell, had been an actor and later became a speech teacher. Alexander Melville followed in his footsteps and worked for many years as a teacher of elocution, which is the art of speaking correctly and effectively. He also studied the way a person uses his larynx, mouth, tongue, and lips to form sounds. After years of teaching and study, Bell invented Visible Speech, a set of symbols based on the position

When he was a teenager, Alexander Graham Bell and his older brother made a "speaking machine" that mechanically produced vocal sounds. A local butcher had given them a larynx from a lamb, and the boys made a model of the lamb's vocal organs. They attached levers that moved the organs. When they blew into a tube, it moved the levers which, in turn, made the organs produce sounds like human cries.

and action of the throat, tongue, and lips while making sounds. This technique would later be used in the education of the deaf.

Eliza Grace, the daughter of a surgeon in the Royal Navy, was an accomplished pianist despite the fact that she was hearing impaired. She was able to hear some sounds with the use of a speaking tube. She was Alexander Graham's first and most important teacher.

In 1865, the Bell family moved to London where Alexander Melville continued the work begun by his father who had recently died. In London, Alexander Graham became his father's assistant and studied anatomy and physiology at University College. He also began experimenting with the transmission of sounds using his family's piano and tuning forks. But his discoveries would soon be placed on hold. By 1870, both of his brothers had died of tuberculosis, and his father persuaded his family to move to Brantford, Ontario, Canada, where he considered the climate to be better for their health.

Alexander Melville had become well known for his work with Visible Speech, and when he was invited to introduce this technique to Sarah Fuller's School for the Deaf in Boston, he instead sent his partner and son, Alexander Graham. From then on, Alexander Graham Bell dedicated his life to teaching the deaf and developing new instruments for their use. He visited various schools for the deaf in the Boston area, and in 1873, he became professor of vocal physiology and the mechanics of speech. He presented lectures at Boston University and the University of Oxford.

Bell also began to take private deaf students. From 1873 until 1876, Bell had the sole responsibility of educating the five-year-old, deaf son of Thomas Sanders in Haverhill, Massachusetts. Sanders would later become treasurer of the Bell Telephone Company. At the same time, Bell met another influential man, Gardiner G. Hubbard, who also had a deaf child and was dedicated to her education. Hubbard later became trustee of the Bell Telephone Company. On July 11, 1877, Bell, a slender, dark-haired young man, married Hubbard's eighteen-year-old daughter, Mabel, who had been deaf since early childhood.

A Man of Inventions

Thomas Sanders and Gardiner Hubbard were so impressed with Bell, they encouraged him to pursue his ideas and continue with his experiments. And they gave him the money to do it. At that time, Bell worked mostly on three kinds of equipment: a phonoautograph, a device that would help a deaf person see a sound; a multiple telegraph, a device that could transmit two or more messages over wire at the same time; and an electric speaking telegraph, or telephone.

All of the experiences he had prior to 1876, led Bell to one of the greatest inventions in history. He had a special ear for pitch and tones, thanks to music lessons with his mother; he had a mind for science like his father and grandfather; and he had knowledge gained from his experiments with the telegraph and other sound-producing devices. Bell developed a basic concept for the phone and worked diligently for over a year to get it to work. Finally, he discovered that he could reproduce the tone and overtones of the human voice through a wire.

Bell gave the plans to build the first telephone to his assistant, Thomas A. Watson (1854–1934), and on March 10, 1876, they used the phone to communicate for the first time. Two months later, Bell introduced the telephone to the scientific world at the Academy of Arts and Sciences in Boston. By July 1877, the Bell Telephone Company was formed and the first telephone was installed in a private home.

Bell continued experimenting with communication equipment and developed many noteworthy devices including the photophone, a device that transmits sound on a beam of light. The photophone was the predecessor of today's optical fiber systems. He also worked on an audiometer, an instrument used to measure how well a person hears, and the first successful phonograph record.

Beginning in 1895, Bell's scientific interests moved into the area of aviation. He worked with a friend, Samuel P. Langley,

Patricia F. Russo: Lucent's New Leader

Taking over a failing company is not a job many want. After losing $16 million and 90 percent of its stock value, one of Lucent's goals for 2002 was to find a leader who would help them at least break even. The company found just the person to fill the job: Patricia F. Russo

Russo was born in New Jersey, one of seven children. "In a big family, everyone pitches in," she said in a 2002 *Wall Street Journal* interview. She attended college at Georgetown University in Washington, D.C., completed the Advanced Management Program at Harvard University, and received an Honorary Doctorate in Entrepreneurial Studies from Columbia College in South Carolina.

Patricia F. Russo.
Reproduced by permission of AP/Wide World Photos.

on things like gunpowder rockets and the rotating blades of helicopters. Bell eventually received five patents for aerial vehicles and four for a system called hydrodynamics, which propels a vehicle by skimming the surface of water.

After the Phone

Bell, his wife, and two daughters moved from Boston to Washington, D.C., in 1882, where he became a United States citizen. By this time, he had become a stout man with a full, gray beard, reminiscent of Santa Claus. And, just like Santa, his benevolent acts continued throughout his lifetime.

He was partly responsible for ensuring the advancement of science and Bell continued research to benefit the deaf. He helped develop the journal *Science* in 1880, became president

Russo began her business career in sales and marketing at IBM, one of the leading technology companies in the world. Although she majored in political science and history, not computer science, she was able to successfully sell mainframes and other computer equipment. At the time, she was one of only a few women who held this type of job. In 1981, she joined AT&T as a manager, and from 1992 through 1996, she was president of AT&T's Business Communications Systems division.

In 1996, Russo was one of the founding executives who helped launch Lucent Technologies. She remained at Lucent for the next five years. From 2001 to 2002, Russo was president and chief operating officer (COO) of **Eastman Kodak Company** (see entry). She returned to Lucent in January 2002, as president and CEO.

After it was announced that Russo would fill the job as leader of Lucent, she said that she would focus on employee morale and building customer relationships. In a 2002 *Wall Street Journal* article, the authors said, "The fact that Ms. Russo has played golf since she was a teenager probably doesn't hurt her sales pitch. Nor does the fact that she knows her customers extremely well." Russo was named one of the "50 Most Powerful Women in American Business" by *Fortune* magazine in 1998, 1999, and 2001.

of the American Association for the Promotion of the Teaching of Speech to the Deaf in 1890, joined the board of the Smithsonian Institution in 1898, served as president of the National Geographic Society from 1898 to 1903, succeeding his father-in-law, Gardiner Hubbard, who was founder of the society, and organized the Aerial Experiment Association in 1907.

During most of his later years, Bell and his family spent increasingly more time at a Baddeck, Nova Scotia, summer home they had purchased in 1886. Eventually they lived there year-round. Bell continued his work, often working and studying past midnight, enjoying the solitude of the quiet hours when everyone else was asleep. He died there at the age of seventy-five.

Alexander Graham Bell will always be remembered as the inventor of the telephone. But his life and works reached far beyond that. For his two daughters, nine grandchildren, and the countless numbers of deaf and hearing children who crossed his path, perhaps he was also remembered as a kind soul and a good teacher.

For More Information

Books

Adams, Stephen B., and Orville R. Butler. *Manufacturing the Future: A History of Western Electric*. Cambridge and New York: Cambridge University Press, 1999.

Grosvenor, Edwin S., and Morgan Wesson. *Alexander Graham Bell: The Life and Times of the Man Who Invented the Telephone*. New York: Harry Abrams, Inc., 1997.

Periodicals

Berman, Dennis K., and Joann S. Lublin. "Russo's Goal as Lucent's New Chief: Restore Luster." *The Wall Street Journal* (January 8, 2002): pB1.

Bruce, Robert V., and Ira Block. "Alexander Graham Bell." *National Geographic* (September 1988): p. 358.

Chang, Kenneth. "The Precursor to Tiniest Chip is Developed." *New York Times* (October 18, 2001): p. A22.

Peraino, Kevin. "An Earlier ATT Spinoff Sputters: Once a High Flier, Lucent Hits a Downdraft." *Newsweek* (November 6, 2000): p 53.

"Telecom: $3-billion Stock Offering, Part of Plan to Split AT&T, Gives Equipment Firm a Value of About $15 million." *Los Angeles Times* (April 4, 1996): p. D-1.

"Telephones in the United States." *Popular Mechanics* (March 2002): pS6.

Web Sites

"The Alexander Graham Bell Family Papers in the Library of Congress 1862–1939" [On-line] http://memory.loc.gov/ammem/bellhtml/bell-home.html (accessed on August 15, 2002).

AT&T. [On-line] http://www.att.com (accessed on August 15, 2002).

Lucent Technologies. [On-line] http://www.lucent.com (accessed on August 15, 2002).

Index

Boldface type indicates volume numbers and entries and their inclusive page numbers;

(ill.) indicates illustrations and photographs.

Sculley, John, **1:** 47, 52

Secure sockets layer, **1:** 4

Servers (computer), **1:** 140–141

Service Quality Indicator (SQI), **1:** 213

Sesame Street (television program), **3:** 527–533, 530 (ill.), 532 (ill.), 536–538

Sesame Workshop, 3: 526–540, 530 (ill.), 532 (ill.)

Sex discrimination, **2:** 338

Shansby Group, **1:** 197–198

Shipping services

American Express, **1:** 15–20

Fargo, William and, **1:** 15–18, 25–26

Wells, Fargo & Company, **1:** 18, 20

Wells, Henry and, **1:** 15–18, 19–20, 25–26

See also Express shipping; Ground shipping

Shoes. *See* Footwear

Shortening, vegetable-based, **3:** 516–517

Shrek (movie), **1:** 156

Siegl, Zev, **3:** 542–544

Sigoloff, Sandy, **2:** 332–333

Sigrist, Lydia, **2:** 276

Silicon Valley, **2:** 321

Skating, ice, **3:** 605

Skull and Bones club, **1:** 217

Slave labor, **2:** 310

Sloan, Alfred P., **2:** 267

Smart Chip, **1:** 22

Smith, Fred, 1: 209–211, **216–220,** 216 (ill.)

Smith, Jack, 2: 272–278, 272 (ill.)

Smith, Robert B., **2:** 270

Snack bars, **2:** 353

Snack food companies

Frito-Lay Company, **3:** 508

PepsiCo, Inc., **3:** 498–510

Snow White (movie), **3:** 624, 625 (ill.), 634

Soap operas, **3:** 517

Soaps, **3:** 511–525

Social responsibilities

Ben & Jerry's, **1:** 72, 76, 79

Carnegie, Andrew and, **3:** 593

Eddie Bauer, **1:** 187

Levi Strauss and, **2:** 378

Starbucks, **3:** 547, 549

Vera Wang, **3:** 602

Soft drink companies

Coca-Cola, **1:** 104–119, 104 (ill.), 110 (ill.), 111 (ill.)

PepsiCo, **3:** 498–510, 498 (ill.), 501 (ill.), 502 (ill.)

Software developers

Microsoft, **3:** 442–456, 449 (ill.)

Netscape, **3:** 471–484

Songwriting, **3:** 466–467

Sonic Cruiser, **1:** 95

Soviet Union, **3:** 507, 509

Soybeans, **1:** 236

Speaking machines, **2:** 410

Speedee Service System, **3:** 428

Spiegel Inc., **1:** 186, 187–188

Spielberg, Steven, 1: 149, 150–152, 152 (ill.), 154 (ill.), 155, **158–166,** 158 (ill.)

Spirituality, **2:** 303–304

Sponsorships

Eddie Bauer, Inc., **1:** 187

Nike, Inc., **3:** 490

Sporting goods companies

Eddie Bauer, Inc., **1:** 181–193, 185 (ill.)

L. L. Bean, **2:** 387–400, 387 (ill.), 390 (ill.), 392 (ill.), 394 (ill.)

Nike, Inc., **3:** 485–497

Sports teams, **1:** 37, **3:** 629

Sports utility vehicles (SUVs)

Eddie Bauer, Inc. and, **1:** 185–186

L. L. Bean and, **2:** 394–395

Spreadsheets, **3:** 446

SQI (Service Quality Indicator), **1:** 213

S. S. Kresge Corporation, **2:** 362–364, 371

See also Kmart Corporation

SST (Supersonic transport), **1:** 93

Starbucks Corporation, 3: 541–555, 541 (ill.), 545 (ill.), 546 (ill.), 548 (ill.), 550 (ill.)

Starbucks Foundation, **3:** 547, 549

Steamboat Willie (cartoon), **3:** 623

Steel manufacturers, **3:** 584–597, 588 (ill.), 591 (ill.)

Steele, Alfred N., **3:** 501

Stempel, Robert, **2:** 270, 276

Stern, David, **2:** 382

Topfer, Mort, **1:** 146
Toyota Motor Corporation, **2:** 274–275
Trademarks
   Nike, **3:** 492
   Procter & Gamble, **3:** 514
Transistors, **2:** 404
Transportation. *See* Air-cargo transport; Automobiles; Shipping services
Travel agencies, **1:** 20–21
Travel services, **1:** 21–22
Travelers Cheques, **1:** 20
Tropp, Barbara, **3:** 423–424
Truck manufacturers, **1:** 221–237, 221 (ill.), 225 (ill.), 227 (ill.), 229 (ill.)
Truman, Harry, **3:** 589
Trusts
   Morgan, J.P. and, **3:** 585
   Standard Oil Trust, **3:** 590
   United States Steel Corporation and, **3:** 585, 586
Tupper, Earl, 3: 570–573, **579–583**
Tupper Tree-Doctors Company, **3:** 580
Tupperware, Inc., 3: 570–583, 570 (ill.), 574 (ill.), 576 (ill.), 577 (ill.)
Tupperware lids, **3:** 573
Tupperware parties, **3:** 572–573, 574–576, 574 (ill.), 581
Turner, Fred, **3:** 440
Turner, Ted, 1: 29, **35–42,** 35 (ill.)
Turner Advertising, **1:** 35–36
Turner Broadcasting, **1:** 29, 37–39
Turner Communications, **1:** 36–37

U

UAW Union, **2:** 267–268
Ulrich, Robert, **3:** 567
Uncle Noname, **1:** 199, 205, 206
Unconditional guarantees
   Eddie Bauer, Inc., **1:** 182
   L. L. Bean, **2:** 388
Unilever, **1:** 79–81, 80 (ill.)
Unions, labor. *See* Labor unions
United Aircraft and Transport Corporation, **1:** 89–90, 99–101

United Auto Workers Union, **2:** 267–268
United States government
   airline industry and, **1:** 90, 99–101
   AT&T and, **2:** 403–404
   General Motors and, **2:** 268–270
   Martha Stewart Living Omnimedia and, **3:** 420
   Microsoft and, **3:** 447 (ill.), 448–449, 476–477
United States Postal Service, **1:** 215
United States Steel Corporation, 3: 584–597, 588 (ill.), 591 (ill.)
Universal Music Group, **3:** 460
University of Oregon, **3:** 494–495, 496
Unsafe at Any Speed (Nader), **2:** 268, 269
Urban decay, **2:** 283–284, 291–292
USX Corporation, **3:** 589–591
   See also United States Steel Corporation

V

Vanderploeg, Watson H., **2:** 351
Variety discount stores. *See* Discount stores; Five-and-dime stores
Vera Wang Bridal House Ltd., 3: 598–609, 601 (ill.), 603 (ill.)
Vera Wang (fragrance), **3:** 604, 607
Vera Wang on Weddings (Wang), **3:** 603, 607
Vertical integration, **3:** 586
Video recorders, **1:** 172
Virtual integration, **1:** 140
Visible Speech, **2:** 409–410
Vivendi, **3:** 460
Vogue (magazine), **3:** 599, 606
Volkswagon Beetles, **2:** 269

W

Wages, at Ford Motor, **1:** 226